If I Gotta Cook
Make It
Quick!
COOKBOOK

BY SHELLEY PLETTL

Creative Ideas Publishing

First Printing 2004

Reprinted 2005

ISBN: 1-930170-14-9   Printed in China

Additional copies may be ordered for $18.95/each, plus $3.50 shipping.

Creative Ideas Publishing
7916 N.W. 23rd Street
P.M.B. 115
Bethany, OK 73008-5135

Order by phone: 800/673-0786
Or by e-mail: cookbooksbyshelley@yahoo.com

Design by Barbara Jezek, Austin, Texas
Production by Kate Withrow, Austin, Texas

TABLE OF CONTENTS

THE AUTHOR

SHELLEY PLETTL has plenty of experience in the kitchen—trying to satisfy the appetites of three very active daughters and a husband who is a speed, strength and conditioning coach for professional athletes. Shelley's love of food and cooking led her into the restaurant business in the Ozarks resort town of Eureka Springs, Arkansas, and the country music center, Renfro Valley, Kentucky.

The Des Moines, Iowa, native gave up the medical field to be a full-time mother and wife. When she is not car pooling everyone to gymnastic meets or swim meets she loves to spend her time collecting recipes, cooking and entertaining family and friends.

This is Shelley's first cookbook, but she had so much fun writing this one, it won't be her last.

INTRODUCTION

THERE ARE MANY THOUSANDS OF RECIPES available today from a variety of sources. A good cookbook is a collection of recipes that are readily available, make delicious dishes, and are quick and convenient for today's cook. In other words, a cookbook that you will use over and over.

If I Gotta Cook Make It Quick contains over 500 quick and easy, hassle free recipes. Everyone-the great cook, the novice cook, the mature cook, the young cook, the hurried-and-on-the-run cook, the "I've got plenty of time to cook" cook-will all find using this cookbook fun and easy.

The kitchen has always been a fertile ground for inventors. Some kitchen devices and appliances have been around longer than you might think. Others are much more recent. On invention may lead to others. Their purpose is to make work easier, quicker, or to make things better. Interesting tidbits about food or cooking inventions are listed at each category divider in this book.

The slow cooker or Crock Pot® has been around for a number of years. It had several years of great popularity, then their use was slow and steady (the way they cook). Suddenly the slow cooker is the current rage, again the "hottest thing in cooking." The modern woman has rediscovered the ease of putting on a meal in the morning and coming home and it is ready to eat. There are many recipes in *If I Gotta Cook Make It Quick* for the slow cooker. Also included is information on how to adapt a regular recipe to the slow cooker.

Some added attractions are a section on substitutions-if I don't have this ingredient, what can I use? There is also a reference section on basic table manners.

Keep *If I Gotta Cook Make It Quick* in a handy place in your kitchen. It just might become your biggest help in putting great meals on the table with a minimum of effort.

ACKNOWLEDGEMENTS

BEGINNING A COOKBOOK can be a frightening experience. My task was made much easier by the support and inspiration of my mother, Sharon McFall, author of four national cookbooks, including the bestseller, *Busy Woman's Cookbook.*

My sister, Linda Burgett, author of a new cookbook called *Mild To Wild,* spent long hours getting my materials ready for the designer. My heartfelt thanks to my two best friends, Mom and Linda.

Thanks to my dad, Gene McFall, for being supportive of my efforts and helping behind the scenes.

My husband Bob, you have been wonderful and understanding when I have had to put in long hours on the book to meet deadlines.

My three sweet daughters, Jessica, Madison, and Emily, thank you for putting up with the inconveniences while I was writing this book, and for being honest judges for my new recipes.

Thank you, Grandma Marie, for teaching me to make the best fried chicken in the world.

My Aunt Pat Howell, a great cook, passed along many of her delicious recipes to me. I appreciate that.

My brothers, Donnie and Scott, SEE, I DID IT!

Thank you, fellow cook, for bringing this book into your home. I hope you find the recipes easy to use and enjoy them as much as I have.

BEVERAGES AND APPETIZERS

INVENTIONS AND FACTS

1. Powdered milk was used in Mongolia in 1200's A.D.

2. Gail Borden got the first patents for condensed milk in 1856.

3. Plastic coated paper milk cartons was invented by Victor W. Farris and were first used commercially in 1932.

4. Iced tea was invented on a hot day at the St. Louis World's Fair in 1904 by concessionaire Richard Blechyden.

5. In the 1800's there were over 185 patents for coffee grinders.

6. George Crum, the chef at Moon Lake Lodge in Saratoga Springs, New York, originated the potato chip to satisfy a disgruntled customer in 1853.

7. Oliver Evans designed the first refrigeration machine in 1805.

8. The first flexible stainless steel, all metal ice tray was invented by Guy L. Tinkhan in 1933. The tray flexed sidewise to eject the ice cubes.

UP TO DATE CHOCOLATE MALT

4 cups vanilla ice cream

1 cup chocolate milk

¼ cup instant chocolate malted milk drink

In blender, combine all ingredients. Cover and blend until smooth. Makes 5 servings.

CHOCOLATE SMOOTHIE

2½ cups milk

½ cup chocolate syrup

½ teaspoon vanilla

1 quart chocolate ice cream

In blender, combine 1 cup milk, syrup, vanilla, and ice cream. Cover and blend until smooth. Add remaining milk. Blend. Makes 6 servings.

CHOCOLATE FIX SHAKE

1 banana, cut in 1-inch pieces

1 cup chocolate milk

¼ teaspoon vanilla

1 cup chocolate ice cream

In blender, combine all ingredients. Cover and blend until smooth. Makes 3 servings.

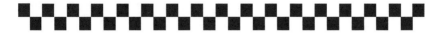

JUST WHIP IT FLOAT

2 bananas, sliced

3 cups milk

1 (10-ounce) package frozen sweetened strawberries, thawed

1½ pints vanilla ice cream

In blender, combine bananas, milk, strawberries, and 1 cup vanilla ice cream. Cover and blend until smooth. Pour into chilled glasses and top with a scoop of vanilla ice cream. Makes 4 to 6 servings.

PEACHY ICE CREAM SHAKE

1 cup milk

1 cup sliced peaches

1 pint peach ice cream

1 teaspoon sugar

In blender, combine ¼ cup milk and peaches. Cover and blend until smooth. Spoon in ice cream, milk, and sugar. Cover and blend until smooth. Pour into chilled glasses. Makes 4 servings.

WHAT A PEACH SHAKE

1 cup sliced peaches

1 cup peach juice

1 cup vanilla ice cream

4 ice cubes

In blender, combine all ingredients. Cover and blend until smooth. Pour into chilled glasses. Makes 3 servings.

DOUBLE FRUIT ORANGE SHAKE

2 cups orange juice

½ cup milk

1 (10-ounce) package frozen sweet sliced strawberries

3 teaspoons sugar

1 cup ice cubes

In blender, combine juice, milk, strawberries, and sugar. Cover and blend until smooth. Add ice. Cover and blend 1 minute. Pour into glasses. Makes 4 servings.

STRAWBERRY SHAKE UP

1 (10-ounce) package frozen strawberries, thawed

1 cup milk

2 cups strawberry ice cream

In blender, combine all ingredients. Cover and blend until smooth. Makes 3 servings.

STRAWBERRY COOLER

1 pint fresh strawberries

½ cup honey

2 cups vanilla ice cream

2 quarts chilled milk

In blender, combine strawberries and honey. Cover and blend until smooth. Add ice cream and 1 cup milk, blend again. In large pitcher, combine strawberry mixture with remaining milk. Makes 8 servings.

COOL OFF ORANGE SLUSH

1 cup milk
½ cup water
¾ cup orange juice
1 tablespoon sugar

In blender, combine all ingredients. Cover and blend until smooth. Pour over crushed ice. Makes 2 servings.

THIRST QUENCHER LEMONADE

1 cup fresh lemon juice
¾ cup sugar
1½ cups cold water
2 (10-ounce) bottles chilled club soda
ice cubes

In large pitcher, combine lemon juice and sugar. Add water and club soda. Mix well. add ice. Makes 5 servings.

TIME SAVER PUNCH

1 (6-ounce) can frozen pink lemonade, thawed
1 (32-ounce) bottle cranapple juice
2 (12-ounce) cans ginger ale, chilled

In large pitcher, prepare lemonade as directed on can. Stir in cranapple juice and enough ice to chill. Just before serving stir in ginger ale. Makes 12 servings.

BRING ON THE PUNCH

1 (6-ounce) can frozen lemonade
1 quart orange juice, chilled
1 quart lemon lime soda, chilled
ice ring (optional)

In medium punch bowl, combine all ingredients. Stir until blended. Makes 17, half-cup servings.

LIKELY TO SUCCEED PUNCH

1 cup sugar
2 cups cranberry juice
½ cup orange juice
2 cups fruit cocktail
4 (12-ounce) bottles lemon-lime soda

In large bowl, combine sugar, cranberry juice, orange juice, and fruit cocktail. Mix well. Pour mixture into ice trays and freeze. Place cubes in bunch bowl. Add lemon-lime soda. Mix. Makes 12 servings.

PUNCH FOR THE HOLIDAY

1 cup Kool-Aid® Tropical Punch flavor sweetened soft drink mix
2 cups water
3 cups cranberry juice
1 cup grapefruit juice
1 (28 ounce) bottle club soda, chilled

In medium punch bowl, combine Kool-Aid and water. Add juices and chill. Just before serving stir in club soda. Serve over ice. Makes 20, ½ cup servings.

HOT APPLE CIDER
(Slow Cooker)

    1 quart apple cider
    1/8 teaspoon nutmeg
    1/2 cup red cinnamon candy

In Slow Cooker, combine all ingredients. Cover and heat on high 1½ to 2 hours until hot. Makes 4 to 6 servings.

DIP FOR FRUIT DIPPERS

    1 (8-ounce) package cream cheese
    1/2 cup crushed pineapple
    1 (7-ounce) jar marshmallow cream
    2 tablespoons orange juice

In medium bowl, combine all ingredients. Beat until smooth. Serve with fresh fruit. Makes 1½ cups.

FRESH SLICED FRUIT DIP

    2 (8-ounce) packages cream cheese, softened
    1/4 teaspoon cinnamon
    1 pint marshmallow cream

In medium bowl, combine all ingredients. Beat until smooth. Serve with fresh fruit. Makes 4 cups.

To keep popcorn, potato chips, and other munchies fresh, store them in the freezer until ready to eat.

FLUFFY FRUIT DIP

1 cup sour cream
½ cup peach preserves
¼ cup finely chopped walnuts
3 tablespoons milk

In small bowl, combine all ingredients. Mix well. Cover and chill. Serve with fresh fruit. Makes 1½ cups.

HOT DIP FOR APPLES

½ cup butter
½ cup light corn syrup
1 (14-ounce) can sweetened condensed milk

In medium saucepan, combine all ingredients, over low heat. Cook until hot. Serve with apple slices. Makes 3 cups.

AMIGO CHILI DIP
(Slow Cooker)

1 (15-ounce) can no beans chili
1 (8-ounce) package pepper cheese, cut into small pieces
½ teaspoon hot pepper sauce
¼ teaspoon garlic salt

In Slow Cooker, combine all ingredients. Mix well. Cover and cook on low 2 to 3 hours. Serve with crackers or chips. Makes 6 servings.

MEXI SPIN DIP
(Slow Cooker)

    2 (15-ounce) cans turkey no beans chili

    1 (8-ounce) package cream cheese

    1 (4-ounce) can diced green chiles

    ¼ cup diced onion

In Slow Cooker, combine all ingredients. Mix well. Cover and cook on low 2½ hours. Serve with chips. Makes 8 to 10 servings.

FIESTA CHEESE BEAN DIP
(Slow Cooker)

    1 (8-ounce) package cream cheese, softened

    1 (15-ounce) can no bean chili

    2 tablespoons taco sauce

    1 cup shredded Cheddar cheese

In Slow Cooker, combine all ingredients. Mix well. Cover and cook on low 3 to 4 hours. Makes 6 to 8 servings.

BEST BEAN DIP AROUND
(Slow Cooker)

    1 (20-ounce) can refried beans

    1 cup shredded Cheddar cheese

    1 (4-ounce) can diced green chiles

    2 tablespoons taco sauce

    ½ cup chopped green onion

In Slow Cooker, combine all ingredients. Cover and cook on low 2½ to 3 hours. Serve with chips. Makes 6 to 8 servings.

ANY NITE PIZZA DIP
(Slow Cooker)

1 (8-ounce) package cream cheese

½ cup pizza sauce

½ cup chopped bell pepper

½ cup shredded Cheddar cheese

1 cup shredded mozzarella cheese

In Slow Cooker, combine all ingredients. Mix well. Cover and cook on low 2 to 3 hours. Serve with tortilla chips. Makes 2 cups.

GOOD TIME PARTY DIP

1 (1-ounce) packet ranch party dip

1 pint sour cream

½ cup thick and chunky salsa

½ cup chopped tomato

¼ cup diced onion

In medium bowl, combine all ingredients. Mix well. Serve with chips. Makes 4 to 6 servings.

A SALSA DIP
(Slow Cooker or Microwave)

1 (16-ounce) package Velveeta® cheese, cubed

1 (8-ounce) jar salsa

In slow cooker combine all ingredients. Mix well. Cover and cook on low 2 hours. Can be microwaved until melted. Serve with tortilla chips. Makes 3 cups.

NACHO MUNCHIE

1 (16-ounce) can refried beans
¾ cup chunky salsa
tortilla chips
2 cups shredded Cheddar cheese

In medium bowl, combine refried beans and salsa. Mix well. On microwave safe platter, arrange tortilla chips in single layer. Spread half of mixture on chips. Sprinkle with 1 cup cheese. Microwave on high until cheese melts. Repeat process with remaining ingredients. Makes 6 servings.

SPINACH BOWL DIP

1 (10-ounce) package frozen spinach
1 cup sour cream
½ cup Miracle Whip®
1 cup chopped green onion

Cook spinach according to package directions. Drain well. In medium bowl, mash spinach. Add sour cream, Miracle Whip, and onions. Mix well. Cover and chill 5 hours before serving. Serve with vegetables. Makes 3 cups.

ITALIAN VEGGIE DIP

1 cup Miracle Whip®
½ cup sour cream
1 (1-ounce) envelope zesty Italian salad dressing
½ cup diced green pepper

In small bowl, combine all ingredients. Mix well. Cover and chill. Makes 2 cups.

FOR CRISP VEGGIES DIP

1 cup Miracle Whip®
2 cups sour cream
4 teaspoons minced onion
4 teaspoons dill weed

In medium bowl, combine all ingredients. Mix well. Cover and chill several hours or overnight. Serve with vegetables. Makes 3 cups.

HOT CRABBY DIP
(Slow Cooker)

¾ cup mayonnaise
1 (8-ounce) package cream cheese, softened
2 tablespoons apple juice
½ cup chopped onion
1 (16-ounce) package imitation crab meat

In slow cooker, combine all ingredients, mix to blend. Cover and cook on low 2½ to 3 hours. Makes 6 to 8 servings.

A TASTE OF THE SEA DIP

1 (12-ounce) package cream cheese
2 (6-ounce) cans minced clams, drained
1 cup shrimp cocktail sauce
1 (6 ounce) can tiny shrimp, drained

In medium bowl, combine cheese, clams, and ½ cup shrimp cocktail sauce. Beat until smooth. Spread mixture in 9 inch pie pan. Pour ½ cup cocktail sauce over mixture, top with shrimp. Serve with crackers. Makes 8 to 10 servings.

MARINARA SAUCE & CHEESE DIP
(Slow Cooker)

> 2 cups chunky marinara sauce
> 8 ounces fresh mozzarella cheese, cubed
> 2 tablespoons fresh chopped fresh basil leaves
> 2 loaves French bread, cut ½-inch thick, toasted

In slow cooker, add marinara sauce. Cover and cook on low 2 hours or until hot. Add cheese and basil. Cook 30 minutes. Dip bread in sauce. Makes 24 servings.

A MUNCHING ONION DIP

> 1 (8-ounce) package cream cheese, softened
> ½ cup Miracle Whip®
> ¼ cup diced green onion
> 1 teaspoon Worcestershire sauce

In small bowl, combine all ingredients. Mix well. Cover and chill. Serve with assorted crackers or chips. Makes 1¾ cups.

QUICK TO MAKE DIP

> 1 (3-ounce) package cream cheese, softened
> 1 (1-ounce) packet ranch salad dressing

In small bowl, combine all ingredients. Mix well. Serve with vegetables or chips. Makes 4 to 6 servings.

Pretzel sticks make great picks for meatball appetizers.

BROCCOLI CHEESE DIP
(Slow Cooker)

1 (10-ounce) package frozen chopped broccoli, thawed
1 stick margarine
1 small onion, chopped
1 (10¾-ounce) can cream of mushroom soup
1 (16-ounce) package Velveeta© cheese, cubed

In large skillet, combine broccoli, margarine, and onion, over medium heat. Cook 5 minutes. Drain. Pour mixture into slow cooker. Add soup and cheese. Mix well. Cover and cook on low 1½ to 2 hours. Serve with corn chips. Makes 6 to 8 servings.

DIP FOR ANY OCCASION

1½ cups shredded cucumber
1 cup sour cream
½ cup Miracle Whip®
½ cup chopped onion

In medium bowl, combine all ingredients. Mix well. Serve with vegetables. Makes 3 cups.

BIT O BACON DIP

1 (1-ounce) packet ranch party dip
1 pint sour cream
¼ cup bacon bits
1 cup shredded mozzarella cheese

In medium bowl, combine all ingredients. Mix well. Serve with crackers. Makes 4 to 6 servings.

PINEAPPLE CHEESE SPREAD

　　1 (8-ounce) package cream cheese

　　1 (8¼-ounce) can crushed pineapple, undrained

　　2 cups shredded Cheddar cheese

　　½ cup flaked coconut

In medium bowl, combine all ingredients. Mix well. Cover and chill. Serve with crackers. Makes 3 cups.

FIX IN A FLASH SPREAD

　　1 (8-ounce) package cream cheese

　　¼ cup chunky salsa

　　⅓ cup orange marmalade

Place cream cheese on plate. In small bowl, combine salsa and orange marmalade, Mix well. Pour over cheese. Serve with crackers. Makes 8 servings.

HAM N' CHEESE SPREAD

　　1 (8-ounce) package cream cheese with chives
　　　　and onion

　　½ teaspoon mustard

　　⅓ cup diced ham

　　¼ cup shredded Cheddar cheese

In small bowl, combine all ingredients. Mix well. Serve with bread or crackers. Makes 3 or 4 servings.

A QUICK TUNA SPREAD

1 (8-ounce) package cream cheese, cubed

3 tablespoons salsa

1 teaspoon dried minced onion

1 (6½-ounce) can tuna, drained

In medium bowl, combine all ingredients. Beat until smooth. Serve with party bread or crackers. Makes 1½ cups.

HERE'S THE BEEF CHEESE BALLS

1 (8-ounce) package cream cheese, softened

2 tablespoons creamy horseradish

1 (2½-ounce) jar dried beef, shredded

In small bowl, combine cheese and horseradish. Mix well. Roll into ¾-inch balls. Roll balls in beef. Place on plate. Cover and chill until firm. Makes 6 to 8 servings.

PARTY TIME CHEESE BALL

2 (8-ounce) packages cream cheese, softened

2 (2½-ounce) jars dried beef, chopped

1 small onion, diced

1 tablespoon Miracle Whip®

1 cup pecans, chopped

In medium bowl, combine cream cheese, beef, onion, and Miracle Whip. Mix well. Chill until firm. Form mixture into ball. Roll in pecans. Makes 8 to 10 servings.

HAWAIIAN LUAU CHEESE BALL

2 (8-ounce) cans crushed pineapple, drained

2 (8-ounce) packages cream cheese

2 tablespoons minced onion

1 cup chopped pecans

In large bowl, combine pineapple, cream cheese, and onion. Mix well. Cover and chill until firm. Form mixture into ball. Roll in pecans. Makes 8 to 10 servings.

ON A ROLL CHEESE BALL

2 (8-ounce) packages cream cheese

½ cup diced cooked ham

2 tablespoons Miracle Whip®

½ small onion, diced

2 tablespoons milk

1 cup walnuts, crushed

In large bowl, combine all ingredients except walnuts. Mix well. Cover and chill until firm. Form mixture into ball. Roll in walnuts. Makes 6 to 8 servings.

SHORT CUT SUGARED PECANS

2 cups pecans

2 tablespoons butter, melted

1 teaspoon cinnamon

½ cup sugar

In medium saucepan, combine all ingredients, over low heat. Cook until hot. Mix well. Spread on cookie sheet. Cool. Makes 4 to 6 servings.

WARM & SWEET PECANS
(Slow Cooker)

2 cups pecan halves

½ cup butter, melted

½ cup confectioner's sugar

1½ teaspoons cinnamon

¼ teaspoon allspice

In Slow Cooker, combine pecans, butter, and sugar. Mix well. Cover and cook on high 2½ hours. In small bowl, combine cinnamon and allspice. Sprinkle mixture over pecans. Mix well. Spread on cookie sheet to cool. Makes 4 to 6 servings.

PECANS WITH A PUNCH
(Slow Cooker)

¼ cup butter, melted

6 cups pecans

2 teaspoons chili powder

½ teaspoon onion salt

½ teaspoon garlic powder

In Slow Cooker, combine butter and pecans. Cover and cook on high 2½ hours. Stir once during cooking. In small bowl, combine chili powder, onion salt, and garlic powder. Mix well. Sprinkle mixture over pecans. Mix well. Spread pecans on cookie sheet to cool. Store in airtight container. Makes 12 to 16 servings.

 To make limp celery crisp, place it in a bowl of cold water with a sliced potato and let stand for an hour or so.

HIT OF THE PARTY ALMONDS

2 cups whole blanched almonds

3 tablespoons butter or margarine

1 teaspoon celery salt

½ teaspoon chili powder

⅛ teaspoon ground red pepper

In large skillet over medium heat, sauté almonds in butter, 5 minutes or until golden. Drain. In medium bowl, combine celery salt, chili powder, and red pepper. Add almonds. Mix well. Spread on cookie sheet to cool. Makes 2 cups.

SNACK PRETZEL NIBBLERS

5 cups tiny twist-shape pretzels

⅓ cup vegetable oil

1 (1-ounce) package ranch dressing mix

Preheat oven to 325 degrees. In 15½ x 10 ½ x 1-inch baking sheet, place pretzels. In small bowl, combine oil and dressing mix. Mix well. Pour over pretzels, stir to coat. Bake 10 minutes. Cool

RED HOT CHICKEN WINGS
(Slow Cooker)

2½ pounds chicken wings, split and tips discarded

⅓ cup margarine

½ cup cayenne pepper sauce

⅓ cup honey

In large skillet, lightly brown chicken wings in margarine over medium heat. Place chicken wings in Slow Cooker. In small bowl, combine sauce and honey. Mix well. Pour mixture over chicken. Cover and cook on low 4 to 5 hours. Makes 4 to 6 servings.

ALL GONE CHICKEN WINGS
(Slow Cooker)

3 pounds chicken wings, split and tips discarded
1 cup honey
½ cup soy sauce
2 tablespoons ketchup
½ garlic clove, minced

In Slow Cooker, place chicken. In small bowl, combine remaining ingredients. Pour mixture over chicken. Cover and cook on low 6 to 8 hours. Makes 8 to 10 servings.

HOT CHICKEN DIP
(Slow Cooker or Microwave)

1 (16-ounce) package Velveeta® cheese, cubed
1 (10-ounce) can Rotel® diced tomatoes and green chiles, drained
1 (6-ounce) package grilled chicken breast strips, chopped

In slow cooker, combine all ingredients. Mix well. Cover and cook on low 3 to 4 hours or microwave 7 minutes. Serve with tortilla chips. Makes 15 to 20 servings.

MOVE ON TO MEATBALLS
(Slow Cooker)

2 pounds precooked frozen meatballs, thawed
1 cup grape jelly
2 cups cocktail sauce

In Slow Cooker, place meatballs. Add jelly and cocktail sauce. Mix well. Cover and cook on low 2 to 3 hours. Makes 6 to 8 servings.

MEATBALLS FOR A PARTY

1 pound ground beef
½ cup chopped onion
1 egg
⅓ cup dry bread crumbs
¼ cup milk
1 (9½-ounce) jar sweet and sour sauce

Preheat oven to 400 degrees. In large bowl, combine all ingredients, except sweet and sour sauce. Mix well. Shape into thirty 1-inch balls. Place on 13x9x2 inch baking pan. Bake 20 minutes. In large saucepan, combine meatballs and sweet and sour sauce. Heat to boiling. Reduce heat. Cover and simmer 15 minutes. Serve hot. Makes 30 appetizers.

BACON DOGGIE ROLL-UPS
(Slow Cooker)

2 (16-ounce) package hot dogs, cut in half
1 (16-ounce) package bacon, cut in half
1 cup packed brown sugar

Take one piece of hot dog, wrap one piece of bacon around hot dog. Place toothpick through bacon to hold. Repeat process until all hot dogs have been used. In Slow Cooker, place half of hotdogs. Sprinkle ½ cup brown sugar over hot dogs. Add rest of hot dogs. Sprinkle with brown sugar. Cover and cook on low 3½ to 4 hours. Makes 32 appetizers.

BACON WRAPPED SHRIMP

1 (16-ounce) package bacon, cooked but not crisp

20 large shrimp, peeled and deveined

1 (8-ounce) can whole water chestnuts

½ cup teriyaki sauce

½ cup barbecue sauce

Preheat oven to 400 degrees. Wrap bacon pieces around shrimp and water chestnuts. Place shrimp in 8 inch glass pan. Brush with teriyaki sauce and barbecue sauce. Bake 15 to 20 minutes. Makes 10 to 12 servings.

SAUSAGE BACON WRAPS

1 (16-ounce) package bacon

1 (16-ounce) package little smoked sausage links

1 cup packed brown sugar

Preheat oven to 400 degrees. Cut each bacon strip in half. Wrap one piece of bacon around each sausage. Place in foil lined 15 x 10 x 1-inch baking pan. Sprinkle with brown sugar. Bake uncovered 30 to 40 minutes or until bacon is crisp. Makes 3½ dozen.

SWEET AND TANGY SMOKIES
(Slow Cooker)

1 cup currant jelly

1 cup Dijon style mustard

¼ cup ketchup

¾ cup packed brown sugar

4 (16-ounce) packages little smokie sausages

In Slow Cooker, combine all ingredients. Mix well. Cover and cook on low 2 to 3 hours. Makes 20 servings.

A SALSA SNACK

1 (12-ounce) package cream cheese, softened

¾ cup salsa

1 cup chopped tomato

½ cup diced onion

½ cup diced black olives

In a 2-quart dish, spread cream cheese and salsa. Top with tomato, onions, and black olives over mixture. Serve with large corn chips. Makes 6 servings.

HOMEMADE GUACAMOLE

1 large ripe avocado, peeled and seeded

4 teaspoons lemon juice

1 tablespoon diced onion

1 clove garlic, minced

In small bowl, mash avocado. Add lemon juice, onion, and garilic. Mix well. Makes 3 to 4 servings.

BEAN WITH CHEESE QUESADILLAS

1 (16-ounce) can refried beans

½ cup picante sauce

12 (8-inch) flour tortillas

1 cup shredded Cheddar cheese

2 green onions, chopped

Preheat oven to 400 degrees. In small bowl, combine beans and sauce. Mix well. Place 6 tortillas on 2 baking sheets. Spread mixture on each tortilla. Top with cheese and onions. Moisten edges of tortillas with water. Top with remaining tortillas. Press edges together. Bake for 10 minutes or until hot. Cut each into 4 wedges. Makes 24 wedges.

SAN JOSE SALSA

3 tomatoes, chopped

½ (4-ounce) can diced green chiles

½ cup chopped onion

1 clove garlic minced

2 tablespoons hot pepper sauce

In blender, combine all ingredients. Cover and blend just until ingredients are combined. Makes 6 to 8 servings.

BUBBLY POTATO SKINS

6 large potatoes, baked

½ cup butter or margarine

1 teaspoon salt

1½ cups shredded Cheddar cheese

6 slices bacon, cooked and crumbled

Cut each potato in half lengthwise. Using a spoon scoop out potato pulp, leaving ¼-inch thick shell. Brush potato skins with butter. Sprinkle with salt and cheese. Place on baking sheet. Place under broiler until cheese melts. Sprinkle with bacon. Makes 12 servings.

BATTER FOR FRIED VEGGIES

1⅓ cups all purpose flour

1 tablespoon melted butter

2 egg yolks, beaten

¾ cup beer

2 egg whites, stiffly beaten

In large bowl, combine flour, butter, and egg yolks. Mix well. Add beer. Mix until well blended. Cover and chill. When ready to cook, fold in egg whites until lump free. Dip fresh vegetables in batter. Deep fry.

ROLL & EAT PICKLE ROLLS

1 (8-ounce) package cream cheese
1 tablespoon Miracle Whip®
8 ham slices
8 pickles

In small bowl, combine cream cheese and Miracle Whip. Beat until smooth. Spread mixture on ham slices. Wrap ham around pickle. Slice each pickle into 1-inch slices. Place on plate. Cover and chill until ready to serve. Makes 16 servings.

STUFFED CELERY

1 (8-ounce) package cream cheese, softened
¼ cup crushed pineapple
4 stalks celery, cut in half

In small bowl, combine cream cheese and pineapple. Beat until smooth. Stuff mixture into celery. Makes 4 to 8 servings.

STUFFED SHRIMP ON CELERY

1 (8-ounce) package cream cheese
1 (4¼-ounce) can tiny shrimp, drained
¼ cup minced celery
1 tablespoon Miracle Whip®
6 large stalks celery, cut into 3-inch slices

In medium bowl, combine cream cheese, shrimp, minced celery, and Miracle Whip. Beat until smooth. Stuff celery stalks with mixture. Makes 8 to 10 servings.

APPLE SURPRISE

1 (8-ounce) package cream cheese, softened

¾ cup packed brown sugar

1 teaspoon vanilla

6 apples, cut into wedges

1 cup chopped walnuts

In small bowl, combine cheese, brown sugar, and vanilla. Beat until smooth. Spread mixture on apple wedges. Place on plate. Sprinkle walnuts over wedges. Makes 24 servings.

THE BEST DEVILED EGGS
(Busy Women's Cookbook)

6 eggs, hard boiled

⅛ teaspoon prepared mustard

3½ tablespoons Miracle Whip®

1 teaspoon sugar

Cut hard boiled eggs into halves. Slip out yolks. In a small bowl, add yolks, mustard, Miracle Whip, and sugar. Mash with a fork until smooth. Fill egg whites with mixture. Sprinkle with paprika (optional). Makes 6 to 8 servings.

NOTES

SOUPS
AND
SALADS

INVENTIONS AND FACTS

1. The first soup dates back to 6,000 B.C., usually made from hippopotamus or other animal bones.

2. Stephan J. Poplawski invented the blender in 1922.

3. African American inventor J. Thomas White devised the lemon squeezer in 1896.

4. In the 1800's there were over 500 patents for apple-potato peelers.

5. Dow Chemical Company introduced Saran Wrap®, the first cling wrap for household use in 1953.

6. Scott Paper produced the first paper towels in 1907.

7. Architect John W. Hamms built the first kitchen garbage disposal in1927.

8. Henry Wasylyk, a Canadian inventor, developed the green plastic garbage bag in 1950.

STIR-FRY VEGETABLE SOUP
(Slow Cooker)

> 1 pound sirloin steak, cut into ¼-inch strips, browned
> 2 (14-ounce) cans beef broth
> 1 (16-ounce) package frozen stir-fry vegetables
> 3 green onions, sliced
> ¼ cup stir-fry sauce

In Slow Cooker, combine all ingredients. Mix well. Cover and cook on low 3 to 4 hours. Makes 6 servings.

THREE BEEF SOUP
(Slow Cooker)

> 1 cup ground beef, cooked, crumbled
> 1 teaspoon butter or margarine
> 1 (10¾-ounce) can beef soup
> 2 (10¾-ounce) cans beef noodle soup
> 2 cans water

In Slow Cooker, combine all ingredients. Cover and cook on low 1½ to 2 hours. Makes 6 to 8 servings.

BEEF POTATO SOUP
(Slow Cooker)

> 1 pound ground beef, browned
> 4 cups cubed potatoes
> 1 small onion, chopped
> 3 (8-ounce) cans tomato sauce

In Slow Cooker, combine all ingredients. Cover and cook on low 8 to 10 hours or high 5 hours. Makes 6 to 8 servings.

VEGETABLES AND BEEF SOUP
(Slow Cooker)

1 pound ground beef, browned and drained

2 cups tomato juice

2 cups beef broth

1 (16-ounce) package frozen mixed vegetables

In Slow Cooker, combine all ingredients. Cover and cook on low 3 to 4 hours. Makes 4 to 5 servings.

HURRY UP VEGETABLE SOUP

4 slices bacon, cut in 2-inch pieces

¼ cup all-purpose flour

1 teaspoon salt

3 cups milk

3 cups cooked mixed vegetables

In large saucepan, add bacon, cook over medium heat until bacon is crisp, remove bacon. Add flour and salt to saucepan, blend well. Slowly add milk, stir until thickened. Add vegetables and bacon. Cover and cook on low heat until hot. Makes 6 servings.

EASY MINESTRONE SOUP
(Slow Cooker)

2 (14-ounce) cans chicken broth

2 (14½-ounce) cans crushed tomatoes

1 (15-ounce) can kidney beans, drained

3 tablespoons Italian seasoning

1½ cups frozen vegetables

In Slow Cooker, combine all ingredients. Mix well. Cover and cook on low 3 to 4 hours. Makes 4 to 6 servings.

FIX-N-GO SAUSAGE SOUP
(Slow Cooker)

    1 (24-ounce) can vegetable juice
    1 (15-ounce) can chili with beans
    2 cups frozen hash brown potatoes with onions and
        peppers
    1 (8-ounce) package Polish sausage, sliced

In Slow Cooker, combine all ingredients. Cover and cook on low 3 to 4 hours. Makes 4 to 6 servings.

SPICY BEAN & HAM SOUP
(Slow Cooker)

    1 cup cubed cooked ham
    1 cup salsa
    1 (15-ounce) can black beans, rinsed and drained
    1 (14-ounce) can low sodium chicken broth
    1 green onion, chopped

In Slow Cooker, combine all ingredients. Mix well. Cover and cook on low 4 to 5 hours. Makes 4 servings.

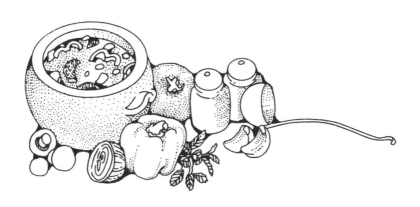

BLACK EYED PEA SOUP
(Slow Cooker)

> 2½ cups black eyed peas, rinsed and drained
> 1 (16-ounce) package turkey sausage, cut into 1-inch slices
> 2 carrots, chopped
> 1 cup water
> 3 (14-ounce) cans low sodium beef broth

In medium saucepan, add peas, cover with hot water. Bring to a boil over high heat. Cover and let stand 1 hour. Drain peas, rinse. In Slow Cooker, add peas, sausage, carrots, water, and beef broth. Cover and cook on low 8 to 9 hours. Makes 6 to 8 servings.

ENCHILADA CHICKEN SOUP

> 1 (10¾-ounce) can fiesta nacho cheese soup
> 1 (10¾-ounce) can cream of chicken soup
> 2⅔ cups milk
> 1 (10-ounce) can white chicken, drained
> 1 (15-ounce) enchilada sauce
> 1 (4-ounce) can chopped green chiles

In large saucepan, combine all ingredients. Mix well. Cook over medium heat until hot. Makes 7 servings.

SHORT-CUT LIMA BEAN SOUP
(Slow Cooker)

> 2 (15-ounce) cans lima beans
> ¼ cup butter
> ½ cup chopped ham

In Slow Cooker, combine all ingredients. Cover and cook on low 2½ to 3 hours. Makes 4 servings.

SPECIAL ONION SOUP
(Slow Cooker)

    3 large onions, sliced thinly
    1 tablespoon butter, melted
    3 tablespoons flour
    1 teaspoon sugar
    4 (14-ounce) cans beef broth

In large skillet, combine onions and butter, brown 3 minutes. Pour mixture in Slow Cooker. In small bowl, combine flour and sugar. Stir in mixture. Add beef broth. Cover and cook on low 7 to 9 hours. Makes 4 to 6 servings.

CREAM OF MUSHROOM SOUP

    2 tablespoons butter
    ½ cup chopped onions
    ½ pound mushrooms, sliced
    2 tablespoons flour
    2 pints half and half
    salt and pepper

In large saucepan with butter, cook onions over medium heat until onions are soft. Remove onions. Add mushrooms over low heat, cook 5 minutes. Add onions and flour. Mix well. Add half and half. Stir constantly until hot. Add salt and pepper. Makes 4 to 6 servings.

To test your kitchen scale, place nine pennies on it. They should weigh one ounce.

MEXI CHEESE SOUP
(Slow Cooker)

2 (10¾-ounce) cans cheddar cheese soup

1½ cups water

½ cup chopped tomatoes

1 (10-ounce) can diced green chiles

½ cup chopped onions

In Slow Cooker, combine all ingredients. Cover and cook on low 2½ to 3 hours. Makes 4 to 6 servings.

CHEESE POTATO SOUP

4 small potatoes

1 small onion, chopped

4 cups water

½ cup shredded American cheese

2½ cups milk

2 tablespoons butter

In large saucepan, combine potatoes, onions, and water over medium heat. Cook until vegetables are tender. Drain. Add cheese, milk, and butter. Heat over medium heat until hot. Salt and pepper to taste. Makes 4 to 6 servings.

BROCCOLI CHEESE SOUP

2 (10¾-ounce) cans cheddar cheese soup

1 pint half and half

½ cup milk

1 (10-ounce) package frozen chopped broccoli, thawed

In large saucepan, combine all ingredients. Mix well over low heat. Cook 15 to 20 minutes. Makes 4 to 6 servings.

CHOWDER WITH SHRIMP SOUP

2 (10¾-ounce) cans clam chowder soup

1 cup corn

2 cups chopped shrimp

1 cup milk

¾ cup half and half

In large saucepan, combine all ingredients. Mix well. Simmer over low heat 15 minutes. Stirring often. Makes 4 servings.

HOMEMADE CHOWDER SOUP

4 slices bacon, cut in 2 inch pieces

½ cup chopped onion

2 (6½-ounce) cans minced clams, drained (reserve liquid)

1 cup finely chopped potato

2 cups milk

In medium saucepan, combine bacon and onion over medium heat. Cook until bacon is crisp. In 1 cup add reserve clam liquid and water to make 1 cup. In saucepan, add clams, clam liquid, and potato. Mix well. Heat to boiling, over medium heat. Reduce heat. Cover and cook 15 minutes. Stir in milk. Heat until hot. Makes 4 servings.

CREAMY AND TASTY OYSTER SOUP

3 tablespoons butter

1 pint oysters, undrained

2 cups half and half

1 cup milk

¼ teaspoon Worcestershire sauce

salt and pepper

In large saucepan, with butter and oysters undrained, simmer until oysters curl. Add half and half, milk, Worcestershire sauce, heat on low until hot. Add salt and pepper. Makes 4 servings.

OYSTER SOUP

1 pint oysters with liquid

1 tablespoon butter

2 cups lowfat milk

⅛ teaspoon cayenne pepper

In medium saucepan, combine oysters with liquid and butter. Cook until the edges of oysters curl. Add milk, heat to just boiling. Sprinkle with cayenne pepper. Ladle into bowls. Garnish with fresh parsley if desired. Makes 4 servings.

AT HOME CRAB COBB SALAD

12 cups torn romaine lettuce

2 (6-ounce) cans crabmeat, drained

2 cups diced tomato

¼ cup crumbled blue cheese

¼ cup bacon bits

Italian or Caesar dressings

Arrange lettuce in large serving bowl. Arrange crabmeat, tomatoes, blue cheese, and bacon bits in rows over lettuce. Just before serving, drizzle dressing evenly over salad. Toss well. Serve salad on chilled serving plates. Makes 6 servings.

CHICKEN CRUNCH SALAD

1½ cups French fried onions

4 cups sliced cooked chicken

12 cups salad greens

1 large tomato, cut into wedges

1 cup Caesar dressing

Microwave French fried onions on high 1 minute. In large bowl, combine all ingredients, except dressing. Toss well. Serve with dressing. Makes 6 servings.

Clean your microwave by placing a wet paper towel in the oven and microwave on high for 4 minutes. When the paper towel cools a bit, use it to wipe the oven clean.

PERK IT UP CHICKEN SALAD

6 cups torn mixed salad greens
½ small onion, sliced thin
1 pound skinless chicken breasts, cooked and sliced thin
Perk Up Dressing
1 cup raspberries

On large serving platter, arrange salad greens, onion, and chicken. Drizzle with dressing. Sprinkle raspberries over salad. Makes 4 servings.

PERK UP DRESSING

¼ cup raspberry vinegar
3 tablespoons cooking oil
½ teaspoon poppy seed
¼ teaspoon salt

In jar with lid, combine all ingredients. Shake well. Drizzle over salad.

CREAMY GARDEN SALAD

4 cups broccoli flowerets
4 cups cauliflower flowerets
1 pint cherry tomatoes, halved
1 cup ranch dressing
¼ cup grated Parmesan cheese

In large bowl, combine all ingredients. Mix well. Makes 8 servings.

CHERRY TOMATO SALAD

3 pints cherry tomatoes, halved
½ cup chopped fresh basil
1½ teaspoon olive or vegetable oil

In large bowl, combine all ingredients. Cover and chill until serving. Serve on lettuce leaves (optional). Makes 4 to 6 servings.

A CHEF'S SALAD

4 cups chopped mixed salad greens
½ cup diced celery
1 cup chopped cooked ham
1 hard cooked egg, chopped
2 tomatoes, cut into wedges
½ cup shredded cheese

In large bowl, combine all ingredients. Mix well. Add dressing of choice. Toss to mix. Makes 4 to 6 servings.

SALAD IN A BOWL

3 cups shredded lettuce
1 honeydew melon, peeled, seeded, cubed
1 (20-ounce) can pineapple chunks, drained
1 pint strawberries, halved
1 large banana, sliced
1 (8-ounce) carton vanilla yogurt

In large bowl, place half of lettuce. Layer fruit on top. Cover with remaining lettuce. Spread yogurt over top. Cover and chill. Toss gently, serve. Makes 10 to 12 servings.

STARR STUDDED SPINACH SALAD

½ small cantaloupe

7 cups torn fresh spinach

1 cup cubed cooked ham

½ cup pecan halves

½ medium red onion, sliced thin

Starr Tasting Dressing

Use a melon baller to scoop out the cantaloupe pulp into balls. In large bowl toss together cantaloupe balls, spinach, ham, pecans, and red onions. Pour Starr Tasting Dressing over top. Toss lightly to coat. Makes 4 servings.

STARR TASTING DRESSING

3 tablespoons sugar

1½ teaspoons diced orange peel

2 tablespoons orange juice

2 tablespoons vinegar

⅓ cup salad oil

In blender, combine all ingredients. Cover and blend 1 minute. Pour over salad.

BITE CRUNCHING SALAD

2 cups fresh cauliflower flowerets

2 cups fresh broccoli flowerets

½ cup chopped red onions

4 cherry tomatoes, halved

Crunching Salad Dressing

In large bowl, combine all ingredients. Mix well. makes 4 to 6 servings.

CRUNCHING SALAD DRESSING

1 teaspoon vinegar
½ cup Miracle Whip®
⅓ cup sour cream
1 teaspoon sugar

In small bowl, combine all ingredients. Mix well. Pour over salad.

CITRUS LUNCH SALAD

1 orange, peeled, sectioned
1 grapefruit, peeled, sectioned
1 mango, peeled, sliced
¾ cup fresh raspberries
Citrus Dressing

In medium bowl, combine all ingredients. Toss. Arrange salad on 4 salad plates lined with lettuce leaves. Serve with Citrus Dressing. Makes 4 servings.

CITRUS DRESSING

2 tablespoons orange juice
3 tablespoons honey
1 tablespoon oil
2 teaspoons poppy seed

In jar with tight fitting lid, combine all ingredients. Shake well. Serve dressing with salad.

COOL-AS-A-CUCUMBER

2 medium cucumbers, sliced thin
1 small onion, sliced thin
½ cup sour cream
1 tablespoon vinegar
1 teaspoon sugar

In medium bowl, combine cucumbers and onions. In small bowl, combine sour cream vinegar, and sugar. Mix well. Pour mixture over cucumbers. Blend well. Cover and chill. Makes 6 to 8 servings.

GREEN BEAN STYLE SALAD

2 cups cooked green beans
2 tablespoons French dressing
2 tablespoons diced onions
⅓ cup shredded Cheddar cheese

In medium bowl, combine green beans, dressing, and onions. Cover and chill 5 hours. Add cheese. Makes 4 servings.

PICNIC BEAN SALAD

2 (15-ounce) cans red kidney beans, drained
4 hard boiled eggs, chopped
½ cup chopped onions
⅓ cup sweet pickle relish
¾ cup Miracle Whip®
2 teaspoon sugar

In large bowl, combine beans, eggs, onions, and relish, set aside. In smaller bowl, combine Miracle Whip and sugar. Mix well. Pour over bean mixture. Mix well. Cover and chill before serving. Makes 6 servings.

EASY SPICY BEAN SALAD
(Mild to Wild Mexican Cookbook)

1 (15½-ounce) can kidney beans
1 (15½-ounce) can garbanzo beans
1 (15½-ounce) can black beans
1½ cups salsa
1 tablespoon red wine vinegar
1 teaspoon celery salt

Drain and rinse all beans, pour into large bowl. Add salsa, vinegar, and celery salt. Mix well and chill. Makes 8 servings.

TORTELLINI STYLE SALAD

1 (9-ounce) package cheese tortellini, cooked
1 cup chopped cooked ham
¾ cup frozen baby peas, thawed
½ cup Swiss cheese, cubed
2 cups ranch salad dressing

In medium bowl, combine all ingredients. Mix well. Cover and chill until ready to use. Makes 4 to 6 servings.

ITALIAN SPAGHETTI SALAD

3 cups cooked spaghetti, rinsed
½ cup shredded carrots
1 cup chopped tomatoes
¼ cup diced onion
1 (16-ounce) Italian bottled dressing

In large bowl, combine all ingredients. Mix well. Cover and chill 3 hours. Makes 4 servings.

ITALY PASTA SALAD

1 (16-ounce) package bow tie pasta
¾ cup olive oil
1 teaspoon basil
1 teaspoon oregano
2 cloves garlic, diced
3 Roma tomatoes, sliced
4 tablespoons grated Parmesan cheese

Cook pasta as directed on package. Drain and cool. In large bowl, combine olive oil, basil, oregano, and garlic, mix well. Add tomatoes, cheese and pasta, mix well. Salt and pepper to taste. Makes 6 to 8 servings.

CHARLIE THE TUNA SALAD

2 (6-ounce) cans tuna, drained
3 hard boiled eggs, chopped
2 tablespoons diced onions
3½ tablespoons Miracle Whip®
lettuce leaves

In medium bowl, combine all ingredients. Mix well. Spoon mixture on 4 salad plates with lettuce leaves. Makes 4 servings.

 To remove onion smell from your skin, wet it and then rub in salt. Rinse and wash with soap and the smell will be gone.

RING-AROUND TUNA SALAD

4 medium tomatoes

1 cup cottage cheese

1 (6-ounce) can tuna, drained

¼ cup diced celery

¼ teaspoon onion salt

Scoop pulp from tomatoes. In small bowl, combine cottage cheese, tuna, celery, and salt. Mix well. Fill mixture in tomatoes. Place tomatoes on plates with lettuce leaves. Makes 4 servings.

QUICK TACO SALAD

1 pound ground beef

1 (1.25-ounce) package taco seasoning

4 cups corn chips

4 cups shredded lettuce

1½ cups chopped tomatoes

1 cup shredded Cheddar cheese

In medium skillet, cook ground beef over medium heat until browned. Add taco seasoning. Cook 3 minutes. Arrange corn chips on 4 plates. Add beef, lettuce, tomatoes, and cheese. Can top with salsa, onions, or sour cream, optional. Makes 4 servings.

IMPRESS THE COMPANY COLESLAW

⅓ cup vegetable oil

½ teaspoon garlic salt

1 (3-ounce) package beef flavored ramen noodles

1 (16-ounce) package shredded coleslaw mix

1 (5-ounce) package sliced almonds

In small saucepan, combine oil, garlic salt, and seasoning packet from ramen noodles, cook over medium heat for 3 minutes. In large bowl, crush noodles. Add coleslaw and almonds. Mix well. Drizzle oil over mixture and toss to coat. Makes 6 to 8 servings.

RED APPLE COLESLAW

3 cups apples, unpeeled and sliced

3 cups shredded red cabbage

½ cup raisins

Coleslaw Dressing

In large bowl, combine all ingredients. Mix well. Pour Coleslaw Dressing over mixture and toss until blended. Cover and chill. Makes 6 to 8 servings.

COLESLAW DRESSING

½ cup Miracle Whip®

½ cup sour cream

2 tablespoons sugar

1 tablespoon vinegar

In small bowl, combine all ingredients. Beat until smooth. Pour over Red Apple Coleslaw.

CHICKEN & FRUIT SALAD

1 pound chicken breast, cooked, sliced thin
6 cups mixed salad greens
1 orange, sliced
1½ cups sliced strawberries

In large bowl, combine all ingredients. Mix well. Pour Fruit Dressing over salad. Toss lightly to coat.

FRUIT DRESSING

3 tablespoons salad oil
2 tablespoons honey
2 tablespoons orange juice

In small bowl, combine all ingredients. Mix well. Pour over salad.

SUNNY-SIDE FRUIT SALAD

1 cup mandarin oranges, drained
1 cup pineapple tibets, drained
1 cup shredded coconut
1 cup miniature marshmallows
1½ cups sour cream

In large bowl, combine all ingredients. Mix well. Cover and chill at least 5 hours. Makes 6 to 8 servings.

To keep your salad tomatoes firm, and avoid a watery dressing, slice tomatoes vertically instead of horizontally.

IS IT SALAD OR DESSERT

1 (4-serving) box strawberry flavored gelatin

2 cups whipped topping

1 cup sliced strawberries

2 small bananas, sliced

½ cup chopped walnuts

In medium saucepan, prepare gelatin according to package directions. Pour in large bowl. Chill until almost set. Add whipped topping, strawberries, bananas, and walnuts. Mix well, but gently. Chill until firm. Makes 4 to 6 servings.

WHAT A COOL SALAD

1 (4-serving) box cherry flavored gelatin

1 cup boiling water

1 (8-ounce) can crushed pineapple, drained

1 quart vanilla ice cream

½ cup chopped walnuts

In large bowl, dissolve gelatin in boiling water. Add pineapple, ice cream, and nuts. Mix well and freeze. Makes 6 to 8 servings.

CHERRY CUTOUTS SALAD

2 (6-serving) boxes cherry gelatin

2½ cups boiling water

1 cup cold milk

1 (4-serving) box instant vanilla pudding mix

In large bowl, combine gelatin and boiling water. Mix well, set aside. In medium bowl, whisk milk and pudding mix, blend until smooth. Pour into gelatin. Mix well. Pour mixture into 13 x 9 x 2-inch dish sprayed with non-sticking cooking spray. Cover and chill until set. Cut into cubes or use cookie cutters to make shapes. Makes 8 to 10 servings.

SWIFT-TO-FIX CHERRY SALAD

1 (20-ounce) can cherry pie filling
2 cups miniature marshmallows
1 (8-ounce) tub frozen whipped topping
1 (14-ounce) can sweetened condensed milk

In large bowl, combine all ingredients. Mix well. Cover and chill.
Makes 8 to 9 servings.

GRAMMY'S CHERRY SALAD

1 (20-ounce) can cherry pie filling
1 (15.25-ounce) can fruit cocktail
3 bananas, sliced

In large bowl, combine all ingredients. Mix well. Cover and chill.
Makes 8 to 12 servings.

RASPBERRY TOSSED SALAD

8 cups torn Romaine lettuce
1 cup fresh raspberries
½ cup seedless raspberry jam
¼ cup cider vinegar
¼ cup honey
2½ tablespoons vegetable oil

In large bowl, combine the lettuce and raspberries. In blender, combine jam, vinegar, honey, and oil. Cover and blend until smooth. Serve
with salad. Makes 10 servings.

RASPBERRY SAUCY SALAD

1 (16-ounce) jar thick applesauce
1 (4-serving) box raspberry gelatin
¼ teaspoon raspberry flavoring
1 teaspoon orange flavoring
1 cup 7-Up®

In medium saucepan, add applesauce, over medium heat bring to a boil. Stir in dry gelatin until dissolved. Add raspberry and orange flavoring. Mix. Add 7-Up. Mix well. Pour into medium bowl. Cover and chill. Makes 6 to 8 servings.

CRANBERRY BANANA SALAD

1 (4-serving) box raspberry gelatin
1 cup boiling water
½ cup cold water
1 (16-ounce) can whole cranberry sauce
2 bananas, sliced
½ cup chopped walnuts

In large bowl, add raspberry gelatin in boiling water. Mix until dissolved, add cold water. Chill until partially thickened. Add cranberry sauce, bananas, and walnuts. Mix well and spoon into molds. Cover and chill until set. Makes 6 to 8 servings.

ANYTIME FRUIT SALAD

½ cup halved green grapes
2 small bananas, chopped
2 cups small curd cottage cheese
¼ cup chopped pecans

In medium bowl, combine all ingredients. Mix well. Serve on salad plates with lettuce leaves. Makes 4 servings.

RICE WITH FRUIT SALAD

1 cup cooked rice
1 cup pineapple
½ cup shredded coconut
2 medium apples, diced
2 cups whipped topping

In medium bowl, combine all ingredients. Mix well. Cover and chill. Makes 6 servings.

ORANGE BERRY SALAD

1 (4-serving) box orange gelatin
1 cup chopped strawberries
2 cups whipped topping

In small saucepan, prepare gelatin according to package directions. Pour into serving bowl. Chill until almost set. Add strawberries and whipped topping. Mix well. Cover and chill. Makes 4 to 6 servings.

EXTRA EASY ORANGE SALAD

2 (4-serving) boxes orange gelatin
1 cup crushed pineapple
1 cup shredded coconut
1 cup chopped pecans

Prepare gelatin according to package directions. Pour into medium bowl. Chill until just set. Add pineapple, coconut, and pecans. Mix lightly. Cover and chill until firm. Makes 6 to 8 servings.

ALMOST DESSERT SALAD

2 (4-serving) boxes lemon gelatin

1 cup boiling water

1 pint orange sherbet

1 (11-ounce) can mandarin oranges, drained, cut in two

1 cup whipped topping

In large bowl, combine lemon gelatin and boiling water. Mix until dissolved. Add sherbet, blend until smooth. Let set 5 minutes. Fold in oranges and whipped topping. Blend. Cover and chill. Makes 10 to 12 servings.

ORANGE SPRINKLE SALAD

2 (16-ounce) cartons cottage cheese, drained

1 (4-serving) box orange gelatin

1 (8-ounce) tub whipped topping

1 (11-ounce) can mandarin oranges

1 (8 ounce) can chunk pineapple

In large bowl, add cottage cheese. Sprinkle orange gelatin over cottage cheese. Fold in whipped topping. Add oranges and pineapple. Mix well and chill. Makes 8 to 10 servings.

QUICK TO MAKE STRAWBERRY SALAD

1 (4-serving) box strawberry flavored gelatin

½ pint strawberry ice cream

1 cup sliced strawberries

In small saucepan, prepare gelatin according to package directions. In medium bowl, combine gelatin, ice cream, and strawberries. Mix gently. Cover and chill until firm. Makes 4 servings.

IT'S A SIMPLE GRAPE SALAD

½ cup sliced purple grapes
2 small bananas, chopped
2 cups whipped topping
¼ cup chopped walnuts

In medium bowl, combine all ingredients. Mix well. Serve on plates with lettuce leaves. Makes 4 servings.

BRUNCH OR LUNCH SALAD

1 apple, unpeeled, chopped
1 carrot, chopped
1 orange, peeled, chopped
½ cup raisins
½ cup Miracle Whip®
1 teaspoon sugar

In medium bowl, combine apple, carrots, orange, and raisins. Mix well. In small bowl, combine Miracle Whip and sugar. Add to mixture. Mix well. Makes 2 to 3 servings

GONE-N-A FLASH SALAD MOLD

2 cups apple juice
1 (4-serving) box lemon gelatin
1 cup chopped apple
¼ cup diced celery
¼ cup chopped pecans

In medium saucepan, bring 1 cup apple juice to boiling. Dissolve gelatin in boiling juice. Mix well. Add remaining apple juice. Chill until partially set. Fold in apple, celery, and pecans. Pour into 3 cup mold. Chill until firm. Makes 6 servings.

MIX AND CHILL SALAD

1 cup yogurt
1 tablespoon orange juice
2 tablespoons honey
½ cup raisins
1 large apple, chopped

In medium bowl, combine yogurt, juice and honey. Mix well. Add raisins and apples. Mix well. Cover and chill. Makes 4 servings.

APPLE CARROT SALAD

3 medium apples, diced
2 carrots, grated
½ cup chopped walnuts
1 tablespoon sugar
½ cup Miracle Whip®
⅓ cup raisins

In large bowl, combine all ingredients. Mix well. Cover and chill. Makes 6 servings.

EVE'S TEMPTING APPLE SALAD

1 large apple, chopped
1 large stalk celery, chopped
½ cup chopped walnuts
½ cup Miracle Whip®
1 teaspoon sugar

In medium bowl, combine all ingredients. Mix well. Cover and chill. Makes 2 to 3 servings.

WALNUT APPLE SALAD

½ cup chopped walnuts

1 medium apple, chopped

2 cups grapes, sliced

⅓ cup chopped celery

1 cup whipped topping

In medium bowl, combine all ingredients. Mix well. Makes 4 servings.

BOWL-OVER APPLE SALAD

2 medium apples, cut into wedges

8 ounces lean cooked beef, cut into thin bite sized strips

2 medium carrots, sliced thin

¼ cup dried cherries

Bowl-Over Dressing

Line 4 plates with lettuce leaves. Arrange apples, beef, carrots, and cherries on top of lettuce. Drizzle dressing over salads. Makes 4 servings.

BOWL-OVER DRESSING

¼ cup apple juice

¼ cup salad oil

2 tablespoons wine vinegar

In small bowl, combine all ingredients. Mix well. Serve over salad.

AUTUMN APPLE SALAD

4 tart green apples, chopped
¼ cup blanched slivered almonds, toasted
¼ cup dried cranberries
¼ cup chopped dried cherries
1 (8-ounce) carton vanilla yogurt

In medium bowl, combine all ingredients. Mix well. Cover and chill.
Makes 4 to 6 servings.

STRAWBERRY VINAIGRETTE DRESSING

1 cup frozen strawberries, thawed
2 tablespoons red wine vinegar
⅛ teaspoon pepper

In blender, combine all ingredients. Cover and blend until smooth.
Makes 1 cup.

VINAIGRETTE DRESSING FOR 4

3 tablespoons vinegar
2 tablespoons sugar
2 tablespoons salad oil
½ teaspoon salt

In small bowl, combine all ingredients. Mix well. Pour over salad or
coleslaw. Makes 4 servings.

GARLIC DRESSING

⅓ cup white wine vinegar
¼ cup salad oil
2 tablespoons water
¾ teaspoons salt
½ teaspoon garlic powder

In screw top jar, combine all ingredients. Cover and shake well.

MUSTARD DRESSING

2 tablespoons salad oil
2 tablespoons vinegar
1½ teaspoons sugar
¼ teaspoon celery seed
⅛ teaspoon dry mustard

In screw top jar, combine all ingredients, cover and shake well.

SALAD DRESSING FOR FRUIT

⅔ cup orange juice
3 tablespoons lemon juice
1 cup sugar
1 egg, lightly beaten

In small saucepan, combine juices, sugar, and egg over medium heat, bring to a boil. Cook 1 minute. Strain. Cover and chill until serving. Serve over fruit salad. Makes 1 cup.

NOTES

MEAT, BEEF, PORK, POULTRY, AND SEAFOOD

INVENTIONS AND FACTS

1. The Humpty Dumpty Drive Inn in Denver, Colorado trademarked the name "cheeseburger" in 1935.

2. Ray Kroc founded the fast food industry with his McDonalds® in 1954.

3. The first drive-in restaurant was in Glendale, California, in 1936.

4. F & J Heinz began selling tomato ketchup in 1876.

5. Since 1868 Tabasco® Sauce has been adding spice to foods.

6. Henry Ford invented the charcoal briquette with the help of Thomas Edison in 1920.

7. Union Carbide manufactured the first green garbage bags for home use in the late 1960's under the name Glad® Garbage Bags.

8. SOS® Soap Pads (Save Our Saucepans) were invented by aluminum pot salesman, Ed Cox, of San Francisco in 1917.

BARBECUE POT ROAST
(Slow Cooker)

1 (3½- to 4-pounds) chuck roast, browned
¾ cup barbecue sauce
¼ cup orange marmalade
1 tablespoon vinegar
½ cup water

In slow cooker, place roast. In small bowl, combine barbecue sauce, marmalade, vinegar, and water. Mix well. Pour mixture over roast. Cover and cook on low 8 to 10 hours. Makes 6 servings.

STEW ON IT BEEF ROAST
(Slow Cooker)

3 to 4 pounds chuck roast
1 teaspoon salt
1 small onion, sliced
1 cup fresh chopped tomatoes
1 (14½-ounce) can stewed tomatoes

In slow cooker, place roast. Sprinkle salt over roast. Cover roast with onions. Add tomatoes. Cover and cook on low 8 to 9 hours. Makes 6 to 8 servings

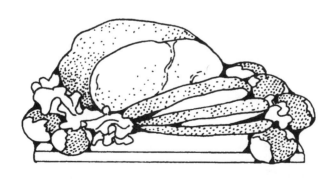

SAUCY ROAST BEEF
(Slow Cooker)

5 pounds roast beef
1 (10¾-ounce) can mushroom soup
1 cup A-1® sauce
1 teaspoon salt
⅓ cup water

In slow cooker, place roast. Spread soup over top of roast. Pour A-1 sauce over soup. Sprinkle salt over mixture. Add water around roast, not on top. Cover and cook on low 9 to 12 hours. Makes 8 to 10 servings

---

FRENCH DIP ROAST
(Slow Cooker)

1 large onion, sliced
1 (3-pound) beef bottom round roast
½ cup water
1 (3.4 ounce) au jus gravy mix

In slow cooker, place onions. Place roast on onions. In medium bowl, combine water and gravy mix. Mix well. Pour over roast. Cover and cook 8 to 12 hours. Note: use broth for dipping. Makes 6 servings.

ROAST AND ONIONS
(Slow Cooker)

3 to 4 pounds chuck roast
1 medium onion, sliced
1 (1-ounce) package dry onion soup mix
2 (12-ounce) cans cola (not diet)

In slow cooker, place roast. Cover roast with onions. Sprinkle dry onion mix over onions. Pour cola over mixture. Cover and cook on low 7 to 8 hours. Makes 6 to 8 servings.

ROAST IN BROWN GRAVY
(Slow Cooker)

2½ to 3 pounds chuck roast, browned
2 (⅞-ounce) packets brown gravy mix
1½ cups hot water

In slow cooker, place browned roast. In small bowl, combine gravy mix and water. Mix well. Pour mixture over roast. Cover and cook on low 8 to10 hours. Makes 8 servings.

PEPPERS OVER STEAK
(Slow Cooker)

2½ to 3 pounds roast steak, cut into serving pieces, browned
1 red pepper, sliced
1 green pepper, sliced
1 yellow pepper, sliced
2 (15-ounce) cans stewed tomatoes

In slow cooker, place steak. In large bowl, combine all peppers and stewed tomatoes. Pour over steak. Cover and cook on low 8 to 10 hours. Makes 6 servings.

STEAK OVER THE TOP
(Slow Cooker)

1½ to 2 pounds sirloin, cut in cubes
1 (10¾-ounce) can cream of mushroom soup
1 (1 ounce) package onion soup mix

In slow cooker, combine all ingredients. Mix well. Cover and cook on low 8 to 9 hours. Serve over rice or baked potatoes. Makes 4 servings.

CREAMY STYLE BEEF TIPS
(Slow Cooker)

2 pounds stew meat
2 (10¾-ounce) cans cream of mushroom
1 can water
½ can evaporated milk
1 teaspoon salt

In slow cooker, combine all ingredients. Mix well. Cover and cook 6 to 8 hours. Serve over rice or noodles. Makes 6 servings.

GLORIFIED ROUND STEAK

1 teaspoon salt
2½ to 3 pounds round steak
½ cup flour
2 (10¾-ounce) cans cream of mushroom soup
1½ cans milk

Sprinkle salt over steak, dredge in flour. Place in large skillet with little oil, brown boths sides of steak over medium heat. In small bowl, combine soup and milk. Mix well. Pour mixture over steak. Cover and cook on low heat 1½ hours. Makes 4 to 6 servings.

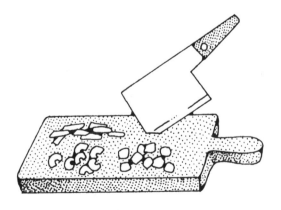

SWISS MINUTE STEAKS
(Slow Cooker)

4 to 6 minute steaks, browned
1 teaspoon celery salt
½ teaspoon red pepper flakes
1 (14.25-ounce) can stewed tomatoes, undrained
½ cup water

In slow cooker, place steaks. In medium bowl, combine celery salt, pepper flakes, tomatoes, and water. Mix well. Pour mixture over steaks. Cover and cook on low 5 to 7 hours. Makes 4 to 6 servings.

STEAK AND TOMATOES
(Slow Cooker)

3 to 4 pounds round steak
2 (14½-ounce) cans chopped tomatoes
1 (8 ounce) can tomato sauce
2 stalks celery, chopped
1 green pepper, chopped

In large skillet with oil, brown steak on both sides. Place in slow cooker. In medium bowl, combine remaining ingredients. Mix well. Pour over steak. Cover and cook on low 7 to 8 hours. Makes 6 servings.

CHICKEN FRIED ROUND STEAK

1½ pounds beef round steak, cut in 6 pieces

2 eggs, beaten

1 tablespoon milk

28 saltine crackers, finely crushed

¼ cup oil

Pound steak with meat mallet to ¼-inch thickness. In small bowl, combine eggs and milk. Dip steak in eggs, coat with crackers. In large skillet with oil, heat until hot. Brown steak on both sides. Reduce heat to low. Cover and cook 20 to 25 minutes. Makes 6 servings.

GLAZED BEEF BRISKET
(Slow Cooker)

1 cooked 3½- to 4-pound brisket

½ cup packed brown sugar

2 tablespoons mustard

1 cup orange juice

In slow cooker, place brisket. In small bowl, combine brown sugar, mustard, and juice. Mix well. Spoon over brisket. Cover and cook on low 2 hours. Baste brisket. Cover and cook 2 hours more. Makes 6 to 8 servings.

To keep a cast iron skillet from rusting, wash it in mild detergent, then dry it by heating it on the stove until all moisture is absorbed. While the skillet is warm, wipe the inside with a wad of waxed

TASTY BEEF FOR BURRITOS
(Slow Cooker)

2 pounds beef brisket

1 small onion, chopped

1 (8-ounce) can tomato sauce

1 (10-ounce) can Ortega® peppers, chopped

1 teaspoon chili powder

In slow cooker, place roast. In medium bowl, combine onion, tomato sauce, peppers, and chili powder. Mix well. Pour mixture over roast. Cover and cook on low 9 to 10 hours. Makes 6 servings.

SOUPED UP MEAT LOAF
(Slow Cooker)

1 (1-ounce) packet onion soup mix

2 pounds ground beef

1½ cups soft bread crumbs

2 eggs

1 cup ketchup

In large bowl, combine all ingredients. Mix well. Shape in loaf. Place in slow cooker. Cover. Cook on low 4 to 6 hours. Makes 6 servings.

NOTE: Can bake at 350 degrees for 1 hour.

paper. Another method is to coat the inside of the hot skillet with a thin film of solid vegetable shortening. Heat the skillet until the shortening smokes, remove from heat and let cool.

MEATLOAF FOR DINNER

1 (10¾-ounce) can tomato soup
2 pounds ground beef
1 (1-ounce) package onion soup mix
½ cup dry bread crumbs
1 egg, beaten

In large bowl, combine ½ cup tomato soup, beef, onion mix, bread crumbs, and egg. Mix well. Shape firmly into 8 x 4-inch loaf. Pour remaining tomato soup over meatloaf. Bake 1¼ hours or until no longer pink. Makes 8 servings.

SHORT CUT MEATBALLS
(Slow Cooker)

3 pounds fully cooked meatballs
1 (1-ounce) package dry onion soup mix
2 cloves garlic, minced
1 (12 ounce) jar beef gravy

In slow cooker, combine all ingredients. Mix well. Cover and cook on low 5 to 7 hours. Makes 6 to 8 servings.

HOMEMADE MEATBALLS

1 pound lean ground beef
⅔ cup grated parmesan cheese
½ cup seasoned dry bread crumbs
½ cup milk
1 egg, beaten

In large bowl, combine all ingredients. Mix well. Shape beef into 20 meatballs. Brown well, drain. Add to your favorite sauce. Makes 20 meatballs.

TASTY HAMBURGERS

2 pounds lean ground beef
1 (1-ounce) package onion dip mix
1 (4-ounce) jar mushrooms, chopped, undrained

In large bowl, combine all ingredients. Mix well. Shape beef mixture into 8 patties. Grill over medium heat 7 to 12 minutes or until done. Makes 8 servings.

IT'S NOT PLAIN HAMBURGER

1½ pounds ground beef
2 tablespoons taco seasoning
¼ cup ketchup
½ teaspoon garlic salt
⅓ cup diced onion

In large bowl, combine all ingredients. Mix well. Shape into 6 patties. Grill or broil 12 to 15 minutes. Serve on buns. Makes 6 servings.

BIG BARN BURGER

1 cup barbecue sauce
2 teaspoons horseradish
1½ pounds ground beef
⅓ cup diced onion

In small bowl, combine barbecue sauce and horseradish. Mix well. Place beef in large bowl, add onions and 3 tablespoons of mixture. Mix well. Shape into 4 to 6 patties. Place on grill. Cook over medium heat, basting with leftover mixture. Cook to desired doneness. Makes 4 to 6 servings.

ONION BURGERS

2 pounds lean ground beef
1 (1-ounce) package onion dip mix
½ cup diced onions

In large bowl, combine all ingredients. Mix well. Shape beef mixture into 8 patties. Grill over medium heat. Cook 12 to 15 minutes. Makes 8 servings.

AMERICAN BEEF BURGERS
(Slow Cooker)

1 pound lean ground beef, browned
2 tablespoons ketchup
1 teaspoon mustard
1½ cups cubed American cheese

In slow cooker, combine all ingredients. Mix well. Cover and cook on low 3 to 4 hours. Serve on buns. Makes 6 servings.

APPLE-ICIOUS PORK ROAST
(Slow Cooker)

2½ to 3 pounds pork roast, browned
1 medium onion, sliced
2 apples, peeled, chopped
3 tablespoons apple jelly
1 tablespoon cider vinegar

In slow cooker, place roast. In medium bowl, combine onion, apples, jelly, and vinegar. Mix well. Pour mixture over roast. Cover and cook on low 7 to 9 hours. Makes 4 to 6 servings.

PULLED PORK WITH ROOT BEER
(Slow Cooker)

2½ to 3 pounds pork sirloin roast
1 large onion, sliced
1 cup root beer (not diet)

In slow cooker, place roast. Top with onions. Pour root beer on onions. Cover and cook on low 8 to 10 hours. Makes 6 to 8 servings.

SODA POP RORK ROAST
(Slow Cooker)

3½ to 4 pounds pork roast
1 teaspoon salt
1 small onion, sliced
1 (10¾-ounce) can mushroom soup
1 (12 ounce) can Pepsi®

In slow cooker, place roast. In medium bowl, combine salt, onions, soup, and Pepsi. Mix well. Pour over roast. Cover and cook on low 8 to 10 hours. Makes 6 to 8 servings.

BBQ BABY BACK RIBS
(Slow Cooker)

¼ cup spicy chili rub
¼ cup packed brown sugar
4 racks, 1 pound each, baby back ribs
½ cup barbecue sauce

In small bowl, combine chili rub and brown sugar. Mix well. Rub mixture over ribs. Curl ribs meaty side out, stand upright on thick ends in 5-to 6-quart slow cooker. Cover and cook on low 8 to 9 hours. Serve with sauce. Makes 4 to 6 servings.

UNBELIEVABLY TENDER CHOPS
(Slow Cooker)

6 pork chops
1 medium onion, sliced
1 (10¾-ounce) can cream of celery soup
¼ cup water

In slow cooker, place chops. Top with onions. In small bowl, combine soup and water. Mix well. Pour over onions. Cover and cook on low 8 to 9 hours. Makes 6 servings.

GLAZED OVER PORK CHOPS

½ teaspoon salt
4 pork chops, 1 inch thick
⅓ cup Dijon mustard
¼ cup honey

Sprinkle salt over chops. In small bowl, combine mustard and honey. Mix well. Brush mixture over chops. Place chops on grill. Cook over medium heat 6 to 7 minutes on both sides. Makes 4 servings.

PORK CHOPS "N" CHILI SAUCE
(Slow Cooker)

4 pork loin chops
1 small onion, sliced
1 small green pepper, sliced
1 (12-ounce) bottle chili sauce

In slow cooker, place pork chops. Top with onions and green peppers. Pour chili sauce over green pepper. Cover and cook on low 4 to 6 hours. Makes 4 servings.

GRILL OR FRY PORK BURGERS

1 pound ground pork
2 tablespoons chopped green onions
¾ teaspoon salt
¼ teaspoon ground sage

In medium bowl, combine all ingredients. Mix well. Shape into 4 patties. Grill over medium heat until done or fry in medium skillet over medium heat. Makes 4 servings.

HOT & SPICY BARBECUE SPARERIBS

1 cup thick 'n spicy barbecue sauce
¼ cup orange juice
1 teaspoon crushed red pepper
3 pounds pork spareribs

In small bowl, combine sauce, juice and red pepper. Mix well. Brush one side of ribs. Place bone side on grill. Cook 5 minutes, turn, brush mixture on ribs. Cook and baste until done. Makes 6 servings.

CHOP STICK RIBS
(Slow Cooker)

3 to 4 pounds pork ribs
¼ cup soy sauce
¼ cup orange marmalade
1 tablespoon ketchup
1 garlic clove, crushed

In slow cooker, place ribs. In small bowl, combine soy sauce, orange marmalade, ketchup and garlic. Mix well. Pour over ribs. Cover and cook on low 9 to 10 hours. Makes 6 servings.

SWEET CHERRY PORK CHOPS
(Slow Cooker)

    4 to 6 pork chops
    1 (20-ounce) can cherry pie filling

In slow cooker, place chops. Add cherries on top. Mix well. Cover and cook on low 7 to 8 hours. Makes 4 to 6 servings.

HASSLE FREE PORK CHOPS
(Slow Cooker)

    4 pork chops, browned
    1 small onion, sliced
    4 potatoes, peeled, sliced
    2 (10¾-ounce) cans tomato soup
    ½ cup milk

In slow cooker, place chops. Top with onions and potatoes. In small bowl, combine soup and milk. Mix well. Pour mixture over potatoes. Cover and cook on low 8 to 10 hours. Makes 4 servings.

PEACH GLAZED HAM

    1 (4- to 5-pound) fully cooked ham
    1 (12-ounce) jar peach preserves
    2 tablespoons Dijon mustard
    2 tablespoons dark brown sugar

Preheat oven to 350 degrees. Place ham on rack in shallow baking pan. Bake 2 hours. In small bowl, combine peach preserve, mustard, and brown sugar. Mix well. Spoon mixture over ham and bake 30 minutes. Makes 8 to 10 servings.

HONEY "N" SPICE HAM
(Slow Cooker)

1 (2½- to 3- pound) fully cooked ham
½ cup Heinz 57® sauce
¼ cup honey

In slow cooker, place ham. Cover and cook on low 4 hours. In small bowl, combine Heinz 57 and honey. Mix well. Baste ham with mixture. Cover and cook 30 to 40 minutes. Makes 4 to 6 servings.

IT'S THE BEST GLAZED HAM

1 tablespoon mustard
1 tablespoon all spice
1 fully cooked 5 to 6 pound ham
¾ cup orange marmalade

Preheat oven to 350 degrees. In small bowl, combine mustard and all spice. Mix well. Score ham. Rub mixture over ham. Place on rack in shallow baking pan. Bake uncovered 2 hours. Spread marmalade on top of ham. Cook 30 minutes. Makes 12 to 16 servings.

NO BAKE GLAZED HAM
(Slow Cooker)

2 to 3 pounds cooked boneless ham
1 tablespoon orange juice
¼ cup honey
⅛ teaspoon ground cloves

In slow cooker, place ham. In small bowl, combine orange juice, honey, and ground cloves. Mix well. Pour mixture over ham. Cover. Cook on low 4 to 5 hours.

SIMPLE COOKED HAM
(Slow Cooker)

7 pound canned ham

2 cups orange juice

1 (20-ounce) can crushed pineapple

3 tablespoons brown sugar

In slow cooker, place ham. In small bowl, combine orange juice, pineapple, and brown sugar. Mix well. Pour mixture over ham. Cover and cook on low 8 to 9 hours. Makes 8 to 10 servings.

FRIED COUNTRY HAM

1½ pounds country ham, cut into servings pieces

1 cup milk

¾ cup flour

¼ cup oil

In shallow dish, place ham, add milk. Let set 30 minutes. Rinse ham. Dredge ham in flour. In large skillet with oil, heat until hot over medium heat. Fry ham until golden brown on both sides. Note: My Mom fries this ham without flour. Make 4 servings.

BBQ PORK CHOPS
(Slow Cooker)

6 pork chops

1 (10¾-ounce) can mushroom soup

1 cup ketchup

1 tablespoon Worcestershire sauce

½ cup chopped onion

In slow cooker, place pork chops. In small bowl, combine soup, ketchup, Worcestershire sauce, and onion. Mix well. Pour mixture over chops. Cover. Cook on low 8 to 10 hours. Makes 6 servings.

SOUTHWEST PORK CHOPS
(Slow Cooker)

6 pork chops, ¾-inch
1 (15-ounce) can Mexican style chili
1¼ cups bottled salsa
1 cup frozen whole corn
2 cups hot cooked rice

In slow cooker, place chops. Add chili and salsa. Cover. Cook on high 2½ hours. Add corn. Cover. Cook on high 30 minutes. Serve over hot rice. Makes 6 servings.

BASTE WITH GLAZE SAUSAGE

1 cup pineapple preserves
1 tablespoon lemon juice
1½ pounds smoked sausage

In small saucepan, combine preserves and lemon juice, over medium heat. Cook until hot. Place sausage on grill over medium heat. Cook 10 minutes. Brush mixture over sausage until done. Makes 4 to 6 servings.

TAILGATING BRATWURSTS

1 teaspoon caraway seed
1½ cups beer
4 fresh bratwurst

In medium saucepan, combine caraway seed and beer. Prick bratwurst with fork several times. Place in mixture. Bring to a boil. Reduce heat. Cover and simmer 10 to 15 minutes. Remove bratwursts. Place on grill. Cook over medium heat 4 to 6 minutes or until golden brown. Serve with hotdog buns. Makes 4 servings.

ITALIAN SAUSAGE IN SAUCE

1 pound hot sausage
½ cup chopped onions
¼ cup chopped green pepper
4 cups spaghetti sauce
¼ cup Parmesan cheese

In large skillet, combine sausage, onion, and peppers. Cook over medium heat 5 to 6 minutes. Reduce heat to low. Add sauce. Cover and simmer 20 minutes. Serve over spaghetti. Sprinkle with parmesan cheese. Makes 4 servings.

EASY CHICKEN CACCIATORE
(Slow Cooker)

2½ to 3 pounds whole chicken
1 (28-ounce) jar spaghetti sauce
1 small onion, sliced
½ cup sliced mushrooms
½ cup sliced green pepper

In slow cooker, place chicken. In medium bowl, combine spaghetti sauce, onion, mushrooms, and green pepper. Mix well. Pour mixture over chicken. Cover. Cook on low 8 to 9 hours. Serve over spaghetti. Makes 4 to 6 servings.

 When preparing stuffing for a turkey, allow one cup of stuffing for each pound of meat. A one pound loaf of bread makes 8 cups of bread crumbs.

CRANBERRY ROAST CHICKEN
(Slow Cooker)

1 (3½-pounds) whole chicken
1 (15-ounce) can cranberry sauce
1 (1-ounce) package onion soup mix
½ cup water

In slow cooker, place chicken. In medium bowl, combine cranberry sauce, soup mix, and water. Mix well. Pour mixture over chicken. Cover and cook on low 9 to 10 hours. Makes 4 servings.

ZESTY CHICKEN BREASTS

4 boneless, skinless, chicken breasts
4 tablespoons margarine, melted
1 (1-ounce) package fiesta herb with red pepper
   soup mix
½ cup plain dry bread crumbs

Preheat oven to 350 degrees. Dip chicken in melted margarine. In small bowl, combine soup mix and bread crumbs. Coat chicken with mixture. Place chicken in 13 x 9-inch baking dish. Drizzle rest of margarine over chicken. Bake 25 to 30 minutes. Makes 4 servings.

SWISS CHEESE CHICKEN
(Slow Cooker)

2 slices bacon

6 boneless, skinless, chicken breast halves

1 (10¾-ounce) can cream of chicken soup

1 (4-ounce) jar sliced mushrooms, drained

3 ounces sliced Swiss cheese

In large skillet, cook bacon over medium heat until crisp. Remove, drain on paper towel and crumble. In same skillet, brown chicken. Place chicken in slow cooker. In small bowl, combine soup and mushrooms. Mix well. Pour mixture over chicken. Cover and cook on low 8 to 9 hours. Place cheese on chicken. Sprinkle bacon over cheese. Cover and cook 20 minutes. Makes 6 servings

ROASTED GARLIC CHICKEN
(Slow Cooker)

8 bacon slices

8 boneless, skinless, chicken breasts

2 (10¾-ounce) cans roasted garlic cream of mushroom soup

1 cup sour cream

½ cup flour

Wrap one slice of bacon around each boneless chicken breast and place in slow cooker. In medium bowl, combine soups, sour cream, and flour. Beat until smooth. Pour mixture over chicken. Cover and cook on low 8 to 10 hours. Makes 8 servings.

GRILLED BONELESS CHICKEN BREAST

¼ cup Dijon mustard

¼ cup lemon juice

1 teaspoon Worcestershire sauce

4 boneless chicken breasts

In medium bowl, combine mustard, lemon juice, and Worcestershire sauce. Mix well. Place chicken in mixture. Let set 30 minutes. Place chicken over medium heat on grill. Cook 4 to 6 minutes on both sides or until chicken is done. Makes 4 servings.

HOT OFF THE GRILL CHICKEN

½ cup Miracle Whip®

¼ cup grated parmesan cheese

1 teaspoon Italian seasoning

4 boneless, skinless, chicken breasts

In small bowl, combine Miracle Whip, cheese, and Italian seasoning. Mix well. Brush chicken with half of mixture. Place chicken on grill. Cook 4 to 6 minutes. Turn, brush with rest of mixture. Cook 4 to6 minute or until done. Makes 4 servings.

SESAME GRILLED CHICKEN

4 to 6 boneless, skinless, chicken thighs

1 cup soy sauce

½ cup pineapple juice

1 tablespoon sesame seeds

Place chicken in large recloseable plastic bag. Pour soy sauce and pine-apple juice into bag. Chill 4 to 8 hours. Place chicken on grill. Cook 5 to 6 minutes on both sides. Sprinkle sesame seeds on both sides of chicken. Makes 4 to 6 servings.

DOUBLE CRISPY CHICKEN

1¾ cups, crushed corn flakes

1 egg, beaten

1 cup milk

1 cup flour

½ teaspoon salt

3 pounds frying chicken pieces

3 tablespoons margarine, melted

Preheat oven to 350 degrees. Pour corn flakes into shallow dish. In small bowl, combine egg, milk, flour, and salt, beat until smooth. Dip chicken in batter. Coat with corn flakes. Place chicken on cooking sprayed cookie sheet. Drizzle melted margarine over top of chicken. Bake 60 minutes. Do not cover or turn while baking. Makes 6 servings.

PECAN CRUSTED CHICKEN

4 (6-ounce) boneless, skinless, chicken breasts

1 cup flour

2 eggs, beaten

2 cups pecans, crushed

1 cup peanut oil

Preheat oven to 350 degrees. With meat mallet, pound chicken until uniform thickness. Dredge chicken in flour, then dip in eggs and coat with pecans. In large skillet with oil, brown both sides of chicken. Place chicken on baking sheet. Bake 7 to 8 minutes. Makes 4 servings

To make ready-to-eat marinated chicken, place marinade and chicken in freezer bags. Shake bag to coat chicken and freeze until ready to cook.

MARINATED CHICKEN

2½ tablespoons oil

1 tablespoon lemon juice

½ teaspoon rosemary

½ teaspoon salt

4 boneless skinless, chicken breasts

In cup add oil, lemon juice, rosemary, and salt. Place chicken in medium bowl. Pour mixture over chicken, turn once. Let set 30 minutes. Broil 10 to 12 minutes, turn once. Cook until no longer pink. Makes 4 servings.

BONELESS CHICKEN BREAST
(Slow Cooker)

4 to 6 boneless, skinless, chicken breasts

½ cup soy sauce

½ cup packed brown sugar

2 garlic cloves, minced

¾ cup tomato juice

In slow cooker, place chicken. In small bowl, combine soy sauce, brown sugar, garlic, and tomato juice. Mix well. Pour mixture over chicken. Cover and cook on low 8 to 9 hours. Makes 4 to 6 servings.

SAUCE IT UP CHICKEN

4 chicken breasts

2 tablespoons margarine

1 (10¾-ounce) can broccoli cheese soup

1 (10¾-ounce) can cream of chicken soup

1½ cups milk

In large skillet with margarine, brown chicken. In medium bowl, combine soups and milk. Mix well. Pour over chicken. Cover and cook on low 60 minutes. Serve over rice or noodles. Makes 4 servings.

ITALIAN CREAMY CHICKEN
(Slow Cooker)

2 pounds boneless, skinless, chicken breasts

¼ cup butter, melted

1 cup cream cheese and chive, softened

1 (1.7-ounce) package Italian dressing mix

½ cup water

Cut chicken breast into strips, place in slow cooker. In small bowl, combine, butter, cream cheese, Italian mix, and water. Mix well. Pour mixture over chicken. Cover and cook on low 7 to 9 hours. Serve over pasta. Makes 4 to 6 servings.

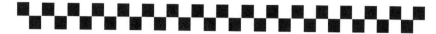

CLASSIC CHICKEN PARMESAN

4 boneless, skinless, chicken breasts

1 egg, beaten

¾ cup Italian seasoned dry bread crumbs

1 (28-ounce) jar pasta sauce

1 cup shredded mozzarella cheese

Preheat oven to 400 degrees. Dip chicken in egg, then bread crumbs. Place chicken in 13 x 9-inch baking dish. Bake 20 minutes. Pour pasta sauce over chicken, then top with cheese. Bake 10 to 15 minutes. Makes 4 servings.

QUICK SUNDAY CHICKEN

1 cup Miracle Whip®

2 tablespoons lemon juice

2 tablespoons honey

1 teaspoon dried basil leaves

3 to 3½ pounds chicken

Preheat oven to 375 degrees. In small bowl, combine Miracle Whip, lemon juice, honey, and basil leaves. Mix well. Place chicken in 13 x 9-inch baking dish. Spread mixture over chicken. Bake 45 to 50 minutes. Makes 4 servings.

A large salt shaker filled with flour can be used to coat chicken or dust pans for baking.

GOLDEN CHICKEN NUGGETS

Oil

2 cups self-rising flour

1 (1-ounce) package ranch dressing mix

2 cups buttermilk

1 (16-ounce) package frozen chicken tenders, cut into
   nuggets

In deep-fryer, fill with oil half it's depth. Heat to 350 degrees. In small bowl, combine flour and dressing. Blend well. Fill another bowl with buttermilk. Coat nuggets in flour mixture, then buttermilk, return to flour. Fry 7 to10 minutes or until golden brown. Drain. Makes 4 servings.

KID'S LOVE CHICKEN FINGERS

½ cup milk

½ cup ranch salad dressing

2 pounds boneless, skinless, chicken breast, cut
   into strips

2 cups bread crumbs

Preheat oven to 375 degrees. In medium bowl, combine milk and salad dressing. Mix well. Add chicken to mixture and coat. Place bread crumbs in ziplock bag. Add half of chicken, seal bag and shake to coat. Repeat. Place chicken strips on a cooking sprayed cookie sheet. Bake for 15 to 20 minutes. Makes 4 to 6 servings.

Add several drops of oil to your skillet when frying with butter to keep the butter from burning.

HOLIDAY TURKEY

20 pound turkey
½ cup butter, softened
2 tablespoons salt
¾ cup hot water

Preheat oven to 350 degrees. Clean and dry, rub butter over turkey. Sprinkle with salt. Pour hot water in roasting pan. Cover with heavy tin foil, seal tightly. Bake 4½ hours. Uncover and bake until golden brown. Makes 10 to12 servings.

TURKEY PIZZA BURGERS

1 (20-ounce) package Italian seasoned ground turkey
1 cup shredded mozzarella cheese
1 tablespoon minced onion
½ cup pizza sauce, warmed

In large bowl, combine turkey, cheese, and onion. Mix well. Shape into 5 patties. Arrange patties on rack in broiler pan or grill cook 4 to 5 minutes on both sides. Put 1 tablespoon of pizza sauce on top of each. Makes 5 servings.

IT'S TURKEY TENDERLOINS
(Slow Cooker)

2 (1-pound) fresh turkey tenderloins
1 cup French salad dressing
2 tablespoons honey mustard

In slow cooker, place turkey. In small bowl, combine dressing and honey mustard. Mix well. Pour mixture over turkey. Cover and cook on low 4 to 6 hours. Cut turkey in ¼-inch thick slices. Makes 4 to 6 servings.

LAMB CHOPS WITH WALNUT GLAZE

4 lamb chops, ¾-inch thick
¼ cup honey
1 tablespoon lemon juice
¼ cup finely chopped walnuts

Place chops on rack in broiler pan. Broil 3 inches from heat 5 minutes. Season with salt and pepper. Turn over. Broil 5 to 6 minutes. In small bowl, combine honey, juice, and walnuts. Mix well. Spoon nut mixture over chops, broil 1 minute.

TASTY CHEESY SALMON PATTIES

1 (14.74-ounce) can salmon, deboned and skin removed
1 egg, beaten
¼ cup buttermilk
⅓ cup self-rising flour
1 cup shredded cheddar cheese
oil

In medium bowl, combine all ingredients. Mix well. Shape mixture into 4 patties. In large skillet, cook patties over medium heat with little oil. Cook on both sides until golden brown. Makes 4 servings.

BARBECUED RED SNAPPER

¾ cup honey barbecue sauce
2 tablespoons lemon juice
½ teaspoon grated lemon peel
½ teaspoon dill weed
2 pounds red snapper fillets

In small bowl, combine barbecue sauce, lemon juice, lemon peel, and dill weed. Mix well. Place fish, skin down on greased grill. Cook over medium high heat, basting with mixture 5 to 7 minutes on each side. Makes 4 servings.

BAKED HALUBUT

6 halibut steaks, 1-inch thick
2 tablespoons margarine or butter, melted
2 tablespoons lemon juice

Preheat oven to 450 degrees. Place halibut in 13 x 9-inch baking dish. In small bowl, combine butter and lemon juice. Pour mixture over fish. Bake 20 to 25 minutes or until fish flakes. Makes 6 servings.

COAST TO COAST FRIED OYSTER

1 pint oysters
1 cup fine cracker crumbs
1 tablespoon flour
1 teaspoon salt
2 eggs, beaten
oil

Drain oysters on paper towels. In small bowl, combine cracker crumbs, flour, and salt. Mix well. Roll oysters in crumbs. Dip in eggs. Roll in crumbs until coated. In deep fat fryer, add oil. Fry oysters until golden brown and crisp. Drain. Makes 4 servings.

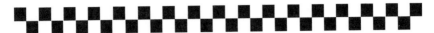

GOOD OLD CATFISH

¾ cup yellow cornmeal
¼ cup flour
1 tablespoon salt
6 catfish fillets
oil

In large shallow dish, combine cornmeal, flour, and salt. Mix well. Wet catfish with water, dredge fish in mixture. In large skillet with 1½ inches of oil, heat over medium heat util hot. Fry fish in batches 5 to 7 minutes or until golden brown. Makes 6 servings.

OVEN FRIED FISH

2 pounds fresh or frozen fish fillets
2 eggs, beaten
1 cup dry bread crumbs
⅔ cup butter or margarine, melted
1 tablespoon lemon juice

Preheat oven to 475 degrees. Dip fish into eggs, then into bread crumbs. Place coated fish in a well greased shallow baking pan. Sprinkle salt over fish. In small bowl, combine butter and lemon juice. Drizzle over fish. Bake until golden and fish flakes. Makes 4 to 6 servings.

To clean cooking spills in your oven, sprinkle salt on it immediately and finish baking. The spillover will turn to ash when the oven cools and can be removed easily.

NEW TWIST GRILLED CATFISH

1 tablespoon lemon juice

1 teaspoon coffee powder

¼ cup melted butter or margarine

¼ teaspoon onion powder

½ teaspoon salt

2 pounds catfish, fillets

In small bowl, combine lemon juice, coffee powder, butter, onion powder, and salt. Mix well. Brush mixture thickly onto fillets. Place on grill. Cook 10 minutes, turn, brush mixture on fish, and cook 10 minutes or until fish flakes. Makes 4 servings.

EASY GRILLED TUNA

2 pounds fresh tuna, cut into 4 servings

4 slices fresh lemon

½ cup ranch salad dressing

Place tuna on heavy foil. Cover tuna with lemon slices, spread dressing over tuna, seal foil. Place on grill over medium heat 20 to 30 minutes or until tuna flakes. Makes 4 servings.

SURF N TURF

2 (8-ounce) lobster tails, split in half

½ cup olive oil

2 teaspoons garlic, chopped

1 teaspoon lemon zest, chopped

In medium bowl, place lobster tails. In small bowl, combine oil, garlic, and lemon zest. Mix well. Pour mixture over lobsters and let set for 15 minutes. Place tails on grill and cook 5 minutes on each side. Makes 2 to 4 servings.

SHRIMP ON THE GRILL

2 pounds fresh or frozen large shrimp, thawed
¼ cup butter or margarine, melted
2 tablespoons lemon juice
⅛ teaspoon hot pepper sauce

Remove shells, devein, and clean shrimp. In small bowl, combine butter, juice, and pepper sauce. Mix well. Thread shrimp on skewers. Brush mixture over shrimp, place on grill. Cook 3 to 4 minutes. Turn and brush with mixture. Grill 4 to 5 minutes. Makes 6 servings.

SKILLET COOKED SHRIMP

16 large fresh or frozen shrimp
½ cup chopped onion
2 cloves garlic, diced
2 tablespoons butter or margarine, melted
2 tablespoons oil

Remove shells, devein, and clean shrimp. In large skillet, combine onion, garlic, butter, and oil. Mix well. Cook over medium heat 2 to 4 minutes. Add shrimp, cook 1 minute. Turn, cook 2 minutes, until pink. Do not over cook. Makes 4 servings.

BAKED STUFFED SHRIMP

2 cups flavored bread crumbs
8 Ritz® crackers, crushed
1 cup butter, melted
15 large shrimp, deveined and cleaned

Preheat oven to 350 degrees. In medium bowl, combine bread crumbs, crackers, and butter. Mix until mixture is firm. With knife, split each shrimp down middle, be careful, don't cut in two. Spread shrimp, put 2 tablespoons mixture in each shrimp. Place on cookie sheet. Bake 8 to 10 minutes. Makes 4 servings.

MADE AT HOME BBQ SAUCE

½ cup diced onion
1 cup ketchup
½ cup chili sauce
½ cup packed brown sugar
2 tablespoons Worcestershire sauce
½ teaspoon dry mustard

In medium saucepan, combine all ingredients. Mix well. Simmer 10 minutes over low heat. Use on chicken, pork, beef, or in beans.

SIZZLIN'S COCKTAIL SAUCE

1 cup Miracle Whip®
¼ cup ketchup
¾ cup chili sauce
2½ tablespoons horseradish
¾ teaspoon salt
1 tablespoon vinegar

In small bowl, combine all ingredients. Blend until smooth. Chill.

HORSERADISH SAUCE

½ cup sour cream
1 tablespoon cream style horseradish
1 teaspoon mayonnaise
½ teaspoon sugar

In small bowl, combine all ingredients. Mix well.

SOUTHWESTERN RUB FOR BEEF

5 teaspoons chili powder
1½ teaspoons oregano
¾ teaspoon ground cumin
2 garlic cloves, crushed
1 tablespoon oil

In small bowl, combine all ingredients. Mix well. Rub on meat, chill 2 to 24 hours before grilling.

MARINADE FOR SEAFOOD

1 cup barbecue sauce
2 tablespoons lemon juice
½ teaspoon grated lemon peel
1 garlic clove, minced
½ teaspoon dill weed

In small bowl, combine all ingredients. Mix well. It is best to marinate fish 15 to 30 minutes.

SPICY MARINADE FOR STEAK

¼ cup soy sauce
2 tablespoons lemon juice
1 tablespoon oil
1 teaspoon ground cumin
1 teaspoon chili powder
1 clover garlic, diced

In small bowl, combine all ingredients. Mix well. Marinate steaks. Cover and chill 3 to 4 hours before grilling. Chill.

VEGETABLES, PASTA, RICE AND CASSEROLES

INVENTIONS AND FACTS

1. French fries were introduced into this country by Thomas Jefferson in the late 1700's.

2. The Swanson® TV Dinner was invented in 1954 by Gerry Thomas. He also gave it the name, TV Dinner.

3. Pasta originated in China about 4,000 years ago.

4. The first cafeteria was opened by the YWCA in Kansas City, Missouri, in 1891.

5. In 1962 instant mashed potatoes were invented by Canadian Edward A. Asselberg.

6. Norwegian Thor Bjorklund invented the cheese slicer in 1927.

7. Chopsticks were developed in China about 5,000 years ago.

8. The dishwasher was invented in 1886 in Shelbyville, Illinois.

CAULIFLOWER MASHED POTATOES

1 medium head cauliflower
2½ tablespoons butter, melted
½ cup cream, warmed

Cut cauliflower into small chunks. Steam until really soft. Pat dry with paper towels. In blender, combine all ingredients. Cover and blend until desired consistency. Season with salt and pepper. Makes 4 to 6 servings.

NOTE: This dish has 6 grams carbs per 1 cup serving.

BABY GLAZED CARROTS
(Slow Cooker)

2 (16-ounce) packages baby carrots
1½ cups water
¼ cup honey
2 tablespoons butter

In slow cooker, combine carrots and water. Cover and cook on low for 6 to 8 hours. Drain carrots and return to slow cooker. Pour honey and butter over carrots. Cover and cook on low 30 minutes. Makes 6 to 8 servings.

SPECIAL SPINACH BAKE

2 pounds
1 (8-ounce) package cream cheese, softened
½ cup butter
¼ teaspoon nutmeg

Preheat oven to 350 degrees. Wash spinach and remove stems. Dry on paper towels. In large bowl, combine cream cheese, butter, and nutmeg, salt and pepper to taste. Fold in spinach. Pour in 2-quart baking dish. Bake 30 minutes. Makes 6 to 8 servings.

COOKING FRESH GREEN BEANS
(Slow Cooker)

2 pounds fresh green beans, washed, snap in pieces
4 cups water
1 teaspoon salt
¼ pound bacon, cut in 1 inch pieces

In slow cooker, combine all ingredients. Mix well. Cover and cook on low 8 to 10 hours or high 3 to 4 hours. Stir occasionally. Makes 6 to 8 servings.

IT'S CALLED SCALLOPED CORN

¼ cup butter or margarine, melted
1 (15-ounce) can corn, drained
1 (15-ounce) can creamed corn
½ cup diced onion
3 eggs, beaten
1 box Jiffy® corn bread mix
½ cup grated Cheddar cheese

Preheat oven to 350 degrees. In large bowl, combine butter, corn, cream corn, onions, and eggs. Mix well. Fold corn bread mix in mixture. Pour into 2-quart baking dish. Bake 40 to 50 minutes. Makes 6 to 8 servings.

TRUE GRILLED SWEET CORN

1 quart water
3 tablespoons sugar
6 to 8 fresh ears of corn with husks

In large pan, add water and sugar. Mix well. Add corn with husks, soak 15 to 20 minutes. Drain corn and wrap each ear tightly in foil. Place on grill 20 minutes. Makes 6 to 8 servings.

UNIQUE CORN BAKE

½ cup chive dip

2 (15¼-ounce) cans whole kernel fiesta corn, drained

1 tablespoon flour

1 teaspoon sugar

1 cup broken corn chips

Preheat oven to 375 degrees. In medium bowl, combine chive dip, corn, flour, and sugar. Mix well. Pour mixture into 2-quart baking dish. Sprinkle corn chips over top. Bake 30 minutes. Makes 4 to 5 servings.

SKILLET FRIED CORN

4 slices bacon

3 cups fresh cut corn

¼ cup chopped green pepper

¼ cup diced onion

In large skillet, cook bacon over medium heat, until crisp, set aside. In skillet with drippings, add corn, green pepper, and onions. Cover and cook over low heat 5 to 8 minutes or until tender. Season with salt and pepper. Sprinkle bacon over top. Makes 6 servings.

CABBAGE IN THE SLOW COOKER
(Slow Cooker)

1 medium head cabbage, chopped

½ cup hot water

4 slices bacon, sliced in half

1 teaspoon salt

⅓ cup butter, melted

In slow cooker, combine all ingredients. Mix well. Cover and cook on low 4 to 5 hours. Makes 4 servings.

BAKED GLAZED SQUASH

1 large squash
⅓ cup water
2½ tablespoons pure maple syrup
1½ tablespoons butter or margarine, melted
¼ teaspoon cinnamon

Preheat oven to 375 degrees. Cut squash in half, discard seeds and membrane. Cut squash into 4 equal slices. Add water in 13 x 9-inch baking dish. Arrange squash in dish. Cover and bake 30 minutes. In small bowl, combine syrup, butter, and cinnamon. Mix well. Uncover squash, pour off water. Pour mixture over squash. Bake 10 minutes uncovered. Makes 4 servings.

SCALLOPED CELERY

3 cups sliced celery
1 cup chopped green peppers
¼ cup diced onion
1 half can cream of celery soup
½ cup cracker crumbs

In large saucepan, combine celery, green pepper, onions, and soup. Cook over medium heat with ¼ cup water. Cook until tender. Drain. Salt and pepper to taste. Pour mixture in cooking sprayed 1-quart baking dish. Sprinkle cracker crumbs over top. Bake 25 to 30 minutes.

SKILLET FRIED CUCUMBERS

3 eggs, beaten
1 teaspoon salt
2 cucumbers, peeled, sliced
1 cup flour
⅓ cup margarine

In small bowl, combine eggs and salt. Mix well. Add cucumbers few at a time to eggs. In small bowl, add flour. Put egg dipped cucumber in flour, coat well. In skillet with margarine, cook cucumbers over medium heat. Cook on both sides until golden brown. Salt to taste. Makes 4 servings.

SLOW COOKING VEGETABLES
(Slow Cooker)

1 (10-ounce) package frozen cauliflower, thawed
1 (10-ounce) package frozen broccoli, thawed
1 (10¾-ounce) can Cheddar cheese soup
4 slices bacon, cooked crisp

In slow cooker, add vegetables and soup. Crumble bacon and sprinkle on top. Cover and cook on low 4 to 5 hours. Makes 6 to 8 servings.

For snow white, cooked cauliflower and potatoes, cook in water that contains a tablespoon of lemon juice.

SUPER VEGETABLE DISH

1 (16-ounce) package frozen broccoli, carrots, and
   cauliflower

1 (10¾-ounce) can cream of broccoli soup

½ cup milk

1 teaspoon soy sauce

¾ cup French fried onions, divided

Preheat oven to 375 degrees. In 2-quart casserole, combine vegetables,
soup, milk, soy sauce, and ⅔ cup onions. Mix well. Bake 30 minutes.
Top with remaining onions. Bake 5 minutes. Makes 5 servings.

JUST LIKE BAKED BEANS
(Slow Cooker)

2 (15-ounce) cans pork and beans

½ cup packed brown sugar

¼ cup diced onions

⅓ cup ketchup

3 slices bacon, sliced in half

In slow cooker, combine all ingredients. Mix well. Cover and cook on
low 3½ to 4 hours. Makes 6 servings.

CAJUN BEANS AND SAUSAGE
(Slow Cooker)

2 (15-ounce) cans pinto beans, undrained
1 pound smoked sausage, cut into 2 inch pieces
2 teaspoons Cajun seasoning

In slow cooker, combine all ingredients. Mix well. Cover and cook on low 4 to 5 hours. Serve over rice. Makes 4 servings.

NOTE: Great with cornbread.

SPICY BBQ BEANS
(Slow Cooker)

1 (15-ounce) can black beans, rinsed, drained
1 (15-ounce) can pork and beans, undrained
½ cup thick n spicy honey barbecue sauce

In slow cooker, combine all ingredients. Mix well. Cover and cook on low 3 to 4 hours. Makes 4 servings.

BBQ FRANKS AND BEANS
(Slow Cooker)

5 beef franks, cut into ½-inch pieces
1 (15-ounce) can kidney beans
1 (15-ounce) can black beans
1 (15-ounce) can butter beans
¾ cup BBQ sauce

In slow cooker, place franks. Rinse and drain each can of beans. Add to slow cooker. Pour BBQ sauce over beans. Mix well. Cover and cook on low 4 to 5 hours. Makes 6 to 8 servings.

ON THE RANCH BEANS
(Slow Cooker)

1 pound ground beef

½ cup chopped onions

2 cups pork n beans

½ cup ketchup

½ cup packed brown sugar

¾ cup salsa

In large skillet, combine beef and onions. Cook over medium heat until beef becomes brown. Drain. Add beans ketchup, brown sugar, and salsa. Mix well. Pour mixture in slow cooker. Cover and cook on low 3 to 4 hours. Makes 6 to 8 servings.

WEEKNIGHT POTATOES
(Slow Cooker)

1 (24-ounce) package frozen hash browns, semi thawed

1 (8-ounce) package cream cheese

1 (1-ounce) package ranch dressing mix

1 (10¾-ounce) can cream of potato soup

In slow cooker, add hash browns. In medium bowl, combine cream cheese, ranch dressing, and cream of potato soup. Mix well. Pour mixture over hash browns. Cover and cook on low 7 to 9 hours. Mix before serving. Makes 4 to 6 servings.

NICE CHANGE MASHED POTATOES

3 cups mashed potatoes

1 cup sour cream

¼ cup milk

¼ teaspoon garlic powder

1½ cups French fried onions

1 cup shredded Cheddar cheese

Preheat oven to 350 degrees. In medium bowl, combine mashed potatoes, sour cream, milk, and garlic. Mix well. Spoon half the mixture
in 1½-quart baking dish. Sprinkle ⅔ cup onions and ½ cup cheese
over mixture. Bake 30 minutes. Top with remaining onion and cheese.
Bake 5 minutes. Makes 6 servings.

SIMPLY A SAUCEY POTATOES
(Slow Cooker)

2 (15-ounce) cans white potatoes, drained

2 (10¾-ounce) cans cream of celery soup

2 cups sour cream

10 bacon strips, cooked and crumbled

6 green onions, thinly sliced

In slow cooker, place potatoes. In medium bowl, combine soup, sour
cream, bacon, and onions. Mix well. Pour over potatoes. Cover and
cook on high 4 to 5 hours. Makes 8 to 10 servings.

*For faster baked potatoes, soak
the potatoes in hot, salty water
for about a half-hour before
baking.*

AU GRATIN POTATOES
(Slow Cooker)

2 (16-ounce) packages frozen hash brown potatoes, thawed

½ cup diced onion

⅓ cup butter, melted

2 cups French onion dip

1 (16-ounce) package American cheese

In slow cooker, combine all ingredients. Mix well. Cover and cook on low 4 to 6 hours. Makes 8 to 10 servings.

QUICK SCALLOPED POTATOES
(Slow Cooker)

4 medium potatoes, cubed and cooked, don't over cook

1½ cups cubed ham

2 (10¾-ounce) cans potato soup

½ cup shredded Velveeta® cheese

½ cup milk

In slow cooker, combine all ingredients. Mix well. Cook on low 3 to 4 hours. Makes 6 servings.

SCALLOPED POTATOES & HAM
(Slow Cooker)

3 pounds medium potatoes, peeled and sliced

1 medium onion, sliced

1 cup shredded Cheddar cheese

1½ cups cubed cooked ham

1 (10¾-ounce) can cream of mushroom soup

½ cup water

In slow cooker, combine potatoes, onion, cheese, and ham. In small bowl, combine soup and water. Mix well. Pour over potato mixture. Cover and cook on high 4 hours. Mix well. Makes 6 servings.

HAM & CHEESE POTATOES

2 cups mashed potatoes

1 cup diced cooked ham

¾ teaspoon garlic salt

½ cup whipping cream, whipped

1 cup shredded cheese

Preheat oven to 450 degrees. In a medium bowl, combine potatoes, ham, and garlic. Mix well. Spread into a greased 1½-quart baking dish. In a small bowl, combine cream and cheese. Mix well. Spoon cheese mixture over potatoes. Bake for 15 minutes or until golden brown. Makes 4 to 6 servings.

Lighter mashed potatoes come from using hot milk instead of cold milk.

OLD TRADITION SWEET POTATOES

2½ pounds sweet potatoes, peeled, cut in half, and cooked

3 tablespoons butter or margarine

¼ cup maple syrup

3 tablespoons brown sugar

1½ cups miniature marshmallows

Preheat oven to 350 degrees. In 8 x 8 x 2-inch baking dish, place pota-toes. In small saucepan, combine butter, syrup, and brown sugar. Mix well. Cook over low heat, stirring frequently 3 to 5 minutes. Pour mixture over potatoes. Bake 25 minutes. Sprinkle marshmallows over potatoes and bake 5 to 7 minutes. Makes 6 to 8 servings.

GLAZED MAPLE SWEET POTATOES
(Slow Cooker)

5 medium sweet potatoes, cut in ½-inch slices

¼ cup packed brown sugar

¼ cup pure maple syrup

¼ cup apple cider

2 tablespoons butter

In slow cooker, place potatoes. In small bowl, combine brown sugar, maple syrup, and apple cider. Mix well. Pour over potatoes. Cover and cook on low 7 to 9 hours. Add butter and stir before serving. Makes 5 servings.

IT'S CREAMY POTATO PATTIES

3 cups half and half
½ cup butter
1 tablespoon salt
1 (24-ounce) package hash brown potato patties
½ cup shredded Parmesan cheese

Preheat oven to 325 degrees. In medium saucepan, combine half and half, butter, and salt, over medium heat, cook until scolded. Place hash browns in 2-quart baking dish. Pour mixture over potatoes, sprinkle cheese over top. Bake 1 to 1¼ hours. Makes 4 to 6 servings.

O'BRIEN POTATOES

4 cups frozen O'Brien potatoes
½ cup ranch dressing
1 cup shredded Cheddar cheese
2 tablespoons grated Parmesan cheese

Preheat oven to 350 degrees. In medium bowl, combine potatoes, dressing, and shredded cheese. Mix well. Pour mixture into 2-quart baking dish. Bake 25 to 30 minutes. Sprinkle with parmesan cheese. Makes 5 servings.

BIG BOY'S MASHED POTATOES

6 medium peeled quartered, cooked potatoes
1 (10-ounce) can diced tomatoes and green chiles
1 cup sour cream
½ cup shredded Cheddar cheese

Preheat oven to 350 degrees. In large bowl, combine hot potatoes, tomatoes, and sour cream. Mash mixture with electric mixer until smooth. Spoon in 2-quart baking dish. Sprinkle with cheese. Bake 5 minutes. Makes 6 to 7 servings.

NO NAME POTATO DISH

½ cup margarine
4 medium potatoes, peeled, cut in small cubes
1 small onion, chopped
8 eggs, beaten

In large skillet over medium heat, melt butter. Add potatoes and onions, cook until golden brown. Add eggs, cook until eggs are set. Stir frequently. Makes 4 to 6 servings.

BAKED POTATOES WITH OUT THE OVEN
(Slow Cooker)

6 to 8 potatoes
foil

Prick potatoes with fork. Wrap in foil. Place potatoes in slow cooker. Cover and cook on low 8 to 10 hours. It's hold about 12. Makes 6 to 8 servings.

NOTE: Do not use water.

A FAVORITE POTATO BAKE

1 (7.2-ounce) package roasted garlic mashed potatoes
1 cup sour cream
1½ cups shredded Cheddar cheese, divided
1½ cups French fried onions

Preheat oven to 375 degrees. Prepare potatoes as directed on package for 2 pouches. Add sour cream and 1 cup cheese. Mix well. Spoon mixture in 2-quart baking dish. Sprinkle with remaining ½ cup cheese and onions. Bake 15 minutes. Makes 8 servings.

GREEN BEAN ALFREDO CASSEROLE
(Slow Cooker)

1 (28-ounce) package frozen cut green beans
1 small onion, chopped
1 cup roasted red bell pepper strips
1 (10-ounce) jar Alfredo sauce
½ cup French fried onions

In slow cooker, combine all ingredients. Mix well. Cover and cook on high 3 to 4 hours, stirring after one hour. Makes 8 to 10 servings.

FETTUCINE ALFREDO

1 (8-ounce) package fettuccine noodles, cooked, drained
2 tablespoons butter
1½ cups heavy cream
½ cup fresh grated Parmesan cheese

In medium saucepan, combine all ingredients. Mix well. Cook over medium low heat 5 to 6 minutes or until heated thoroughly. Makes 4 servings.

CREAMY CHICKEN LINGUINE

8 ounces linguine, cooked, drained
2 cups cubed, cooked, chicken
2 cups cooked mixed vegetables
1 (10-ounce) jar Alfredo sauce

In large saucepan combine all ingredients. Mix well. Cook over low heat until mixture is hot. Makes 6 servings.

LINGUINE WITH SHRIMP

1 pound fresh or frozen large shrimp, peel and deveined
2½ tablespoons olive oil
2½ cloves garlic, minced
½ teaspoon salt
¼ teaspoon pepper
2½ cups chopped tomatoes
1 (8-ounce) package linguine, cooked

Thaw shrimp if frozen. In large skillet, heat oil over medium heat. Add garlic, salt, and pepper. Cook and stir 30 seconds. Add shrimp, cook 5 minutes. Stir in tomatoes. Heat until hot. Add linguine. Mix well. Makes 4 servings.

NOTE: Top with Parmesan cheese if desired.

SHORT CUT LASAGNA

1 (28-ounce) jar spaghetti sauce
6 dry lasagna noodles
1 (15-ounce) package ricotta cheese
2 cups shredded mozzarella cheese
¼ cup grated Parmesan cheese

In 2-quart baking dish, spread 1 cup sauce, top with 3 dry noodles, ricotta cheese, 1 cup mozzarella cheese, Parmesan cheese, and 1 cup sauce. Top with remaining dry noodle and sauce. Cover and bake 60 minutes. Top with remaining mozzarella cheese. Let stand 5 minutes. Makes 6 servings.

ITALIAN MOSTACCIOLE PASTA BAKE

1 pound Italian sausage, cooked drained, crumble
4 cups mostacciole, cooked, drained
1 (28-ounce) jar spaghetti sauce
½ cup grated Parmesan cheese
2 cups Italian style shredded cheese

Preheat oven to 375 degrees. In large bowl, combine sausage, mostacciole, spaghetti sauce, and Parmesan cheese. Mix well. Spoon mixture into 2-quart baking dish. Sprinkle Italian cheese over top. Bake 20 to 25 minutes. Makes 6 servings.

MAMA'S TORTELLINI
(Slow Cooker)

1 pound Italian sausage, cooked, drained
1 (16-ounce) jar pasta sauce
1 (14-ounce) can diced tomatoes with Italian seasoning
1 (9-ounce) package cheese tortellini
1 cup shredded pizza cheese

In slow cooker, combine sausage, pasta sauce, and diced tomatoes. Cover and cook on low 7 to 8 hours. Add tortellini. Mix well. Cover and cook 20 minutes. Sprinkle cheese over mixture. Let stand a few minutes. Makes 4 servings.

MARINARA SAUCE FOR SPAGHETTI
(Slow Cooker)

1 small onion, chopped

4 cloves garlic, minced

2 (14-ounce) cans diced tomatoes with Italian seasoning, undrained

2½ tablespoons tomato paste

1 teaspoon dried Italian seasoning

In slow cooker, combine all ingredients. Mix well. Cover and cook on low 6 to 8 hours Makes 6 servings.

ONE POT SPAGHETTI
(Slow Cooker)

1 pound ground beef

½ cup diced onion

1 cup pizza sauce

1 cup tomato sauce

1 cup chopped tomatoes

1 teaspoon sugar

1 ounce spaghetti, cooked

In large skillet, brown beef and onions. Drain. In Slow Cooker add pizza sauce, tomato sauce, tomatoes and sugar. Cover and cook on low 4 to 6 hours. Add spaghetti, cook 30 minutes. Makes 4 to 6 servings.

 For quick bread crumbs, place two pieces of toast in a sandwich bag and crush with a rolling pin.

KIDS LOVE THIS SPAGHETTI
(Slow Cooker)

1 (28-ounce) jar spaghetti sauce
20 frozen fully cooked meatballs, thawed
3 cups slightly cooked spaghetti

In slow cooker, combine all ingredients. Mix well. Cover and cook on low 2 to 3 hours. Makes 6 servings.

NOTE: If your kids like canned pasta they will love this entrée.

CHICKEN NOODLE PARMESAN

1 (10¾-ounce) can cream of chicken and broccoli soup
½ cup milk
⅓ cup grated Parmesan cheese
3 cups cooked medium egg noodles
2 cups cubed cooked chicken

In large saucepan combine all ingredients. Mix well. Cook over low heat until hot. Stir occasionally. Makes 4 servings.

HOMESTYLE CHICKEN & NOODLES

5½ cups water
5 teaspoons chicken bouillon granules
1 tablespoon butter
2 cups cooked, cubed, chicken
1 (12-ounce) package frozen egg noodles

In large saucepan, add water, over high heat, bring to a boil. Add bouillon granules, stir to dissolve. Lower heat. Add butter, chicken, and noodles. Cook on low 40 to 50 minutes. Add water if needed. Makes 8 servings.

SKILLET CHICKEN 'N NOODLES

1 pound boneless, skinless, chicken breast halves, cubed
1 (16-ounce) package frozen mixed vegetables
1 (10¾-ounce) can cream of chicken soup
⅓ cup sour cream
2-3 cups hot cooked noodles

Spray large skillet with cooking spray. Add chicken. Cook over medium heat until chicken is browned, stirring occasionally. Add vegetables, soup, and 2 tablespoons of water. Mix well. Reduce heat to low, simmer 8 to 10 minutes. Remove from heat. Stir in sour cream and noodles. Salt and pepper to taste. Makes 4 to 5 servings.

NOODLE CASSEROLE ANYTIME
(Slow Cooker)

1 cup uncooked noodles
1 cup cubed ham
1 (10¾-ounce) can cream of chicken soup
1 (8-ounce) can corn, drained
½ cup shredded Cheddar cheese

In medium saucepan, cook noodles until barley tender, drain. Add ham, soup, corn, and cheese. Mix well. Pour mixture in slow cooker. Cover and cook on low 5 to 6 hours Makes 4 to 6 servings.

TUNA & NOODLES FOR SUPPER
(Slow Cooker)

2 (6-ounce) cans tuna, drained
2 (10¾-ounce) cans cream of mushroom soup
1 cup milk
1 cup canned peas
1 (10-ounce) package noodles, cooked, drained

In slow cooker, combine all ingredients. Mix well. Cook on low 4 to 5 hours. Makes 4 to 6 servings.

GRANDMA'S HOMEMADE NOODLES

1 cup flour
2 eggs, beaten
1 tablespoon milk
1 teaspoon salt

In medium bowl, combine flour, eggs, milk, and salt. Place on floured breadboard. Knead in additional flour until dough is stiff. Roll out thin. Let dry for 1 hour. Cut into noodles. Drop into boiling broth. Cook until noodles are tender. Makes 6 servings.

ON A BUDGET MACARONI

½ pound ground beef
2½ cups water
½ cup ketchup
1 cup macaroni, uncooked
1½ cups shredded Velveeta® cheese

In large skillet, brown ground beef, drain. Add water, ketchup, and macaroni. Over high heat bring to a boil. Reduce heat to low. Cover and simmer 8 to 10 minutes. Add cheese. Mix well. Stir mixture until cheese melts. Makes 6 servings.

CREAMY MAC N CHEESE
(Slow Cooker)

1(8-ounce) package elbow macaroni, cooked
4 cups shredded sharp Cheddar cheese
1 (12-ounce) can evaporated milk
½ cup milk
2 eggs, beaten
1 teaspoon salt

Spray slow cooker with cooking spray. In large bowl, combine all ingredients. Mix well. Pour mixture in slow cooker. Cover and cook on low 6 to 8 hours. Note: Do not remove cover while cooking. Makes 4 to 6 servings.

CRUNCHY CHEESERONI

2 cups uncooked, macaroni
1 pound ground beef, browned, drained
1 (10¾-ounce) can tomato soup
1 (10¾-ounce) can cream of mushroom soup
1 medium green pepper, diced
2 cups American cheese, cubed

Cook macaroni according to package directions, drain. In large bowl, combine macaroni, beef, tomato soup, mushroom soup, and green pepper. Mix well. Place half of mixture in 2-quart baking dish. Sprinkle with half cheese. Top with remaining macaroni mixture and cheese. Bake 25 minutes. Sprinkle with remaining onions. Bake 5 minutes. Makes 6 servings.

HECTIC DAY MACARONI GOULASH

1 pound ground beef
4 cups cooked macaroni, hot
1 (15-ounce) can chopped tomatoes
½ cup tomato sauce
salt and pepper

In large skillet over medium heat, brown beef, drain. Add remaining ingredients. Mix well. Cook over low heat until mixture is hot. Makes 6 to 8 servings.

BEEF & MORE MACARONI CHEESE
(Slow Cooker)

1 (7-ounce) box macaroni and cheese dinner
1½ pounds lean ground beef, browned, drained
1 (10¾-ounce) can cream of mushroom soup
1 (15-ounce) can Manwich®

Prepare macaroni according to package directions. Combine all ingredients. Mix well. Pour mixture in slow cooker. Cover and cook on low 3 to 4 hours. Makes 6 servings.

CREATIVE BEEF & MACARONI
(Slow Cooker)

1 pound ground beef, browned, drained
1 (28-ounce) jar spaghetti sauce
1 (7-ounce) package macaroni, cooked, drained
½ cup Miracle Whip®
½ cup shredded Cheddar cheese

In crockpot, combine all ingredients. Cover and cook on low 2½ to 3 hours. Makes 6 servings.

15 MINUTE RICE & BBQ BEEF

1 pound ground beef
½ cup chopped onions
1¾ cups water
1 cup barbecue sauce
2 cups instant rice, uncooked
1 cup shredded Cheddar cheese

In large skillet, combine beef and onions, over medium heat. Cook until brown, drain. Add water and barbecue sauce, bring to a boil. Stir in rice, reduce heat to low. Cover and cook 5 minutes. Sprinkle cheese on top of mixture. Makes 6 servings.

RICE & CHICKEN FOR DINNER

1 (10¾-ounce) can cream of chicken soup
¾ cup milk
1 cup shredded cooked chicken
4 cups cooked quick rice

Preheat oven to 350 degrees. In large bowl, combine all ingredients. Mix well. Pour mixture in 1½-quarts baking dish. Bake 30 to 35 minutes. Makes 4 to 6 servings.

HONEY CHICKEN & RICE DINNER
(Slow Cooker)

2 cups sliced carrots
3 tablespoons honey
½ teaspoon lemon juice
¼ cup orange juice
4 boneless, skinless, chicken breast halves, browned

In slow cooker, add carrots. In small bowl, combine honey, lemon,

and orange juice. Mix well. Pour half of mixture over carrots. Place chicken on carrots. Pour rest of mixture over chicken. Cover and cook on low 6 to 8 hours. Serve over hot rice. Makes 4 servings.

SPECIAL RICE DISH
(Slow Cooker)

1 cup cooked rice

1 (10¾-ounce) can cream of chicken soup

1 cup chicken broth

4 chicken breasts, boneless, skinless, browned

1 (10-ounce) package frozen broccoli, thawed

In slow cooker, combine rice, soup, broth, and chicken. Cover and cook on low 3½ hours. Add broccoli and cook 1 hour. Makes 4 servings.

SO PERFECT ON RICE

1(12-ounce) jar Alfredo sauce

1 (10-ounce) can diced tomatoes with basil

1 pound grilled shrimp

4 cups hot cooked rice

¼ cup Parmesan cheese

In medium saucepan, combine Alfredo sauce and tomatoes. Heat over low heat until hot. Add shrimp. Mix well. Serve on a bed of rice. Top with cheese. Makes 4 servings.

EASY-N-FAST CHICKEN CASSEROLE

4 cups cubed cooked chicken

1 (10¾-ounce) can cream of chicken soup

½ cup sour cream

½ cup butter flavored cracker crumbs

1 tablespoon butter or margarine, melted

Preheat oven to 350 degrees. In large bowl, combine chicken, soup and sour cream. Mix well. Spread mixture in 2-quart baking dish. In small bowl, combine cracker crumbs and butter. Sprinkle mixture over casserole. Bake 30 to 35 minutes. Makes 6 servings.

MEXICAN CHICKEN CASSEROLE
(Slow Cooker)

5 or 6 skinless, boneless, chicken breast

1 (15-ounce) can black beans, rinsed and drained

2 (15-ounce) cans corn, drained

1 cup chunky salsa

1 cup Cheddar cheese

In slow cooker, place chicken. In large bowl, combine beans, corn, and salsa. Mix well. Pour mixture over chicken. Cover and cook on high 3 hours. Sprinkle cheese over mixture. Cover and cook 10 minutes. Makes 6 to 8 servings.

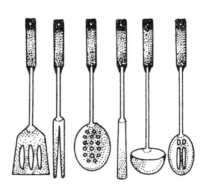

LEFTOVER CHILI CASSEROLE

3 cups corn chips
1 medium onion, chopped
1 cup grated Cheddar cheese
2½ cups chili

In 2-quart baking dish, place half of corn chips. Sprinkle onions over chips. Sprinkle half of cheese over onions. Spread chili over mixture. Sprinkle chips and cheese over top. Bake 20 minutes. Makes 4 to 6 servings.

FIXING CHILI QUICK
(Slow Cooker)

1 pound ground turkey
2 (8-ounce) cans tomato sauce
1 (15-ounce) can red kidney beans, undrained
1 (1¼-ounce) package chili seasoning
1 cup shredded Cheddar cheese

In large skillet, cook turkey over medium heat until brown. Scrape contents of skillet into slow cooker. Add tomato sauce, beans, and seasoning. Mix well. Cover and cook on low 2 hours or high 1 hour. Top with cheese. Makes 4 servings.

To make a funnel for filling salt and pepper shakers, use a clean envelope with the corner cut off.

RUNNING OUT OF TIME CHILI

⅔ pound lean ground beef
2 (14.5-ounce) cans stewed tomatoes, undrained, chopped
¼ cup diced onions
1 (15-ounce) can spicy chili beans, undrained
3 teaspoons chili powder

In large saucepan, brown ground beef, drain. Stir in all remaining ingredients. Bring to a boil. Reduce heat and simmer 5 minutes. Makes 4 servings.

AFTER THE GAME CHILI
(Slow Cooker)

2 pounds boneless, skinless, chicken thighs
2 (14½-ounce) cans diced tomatoes with green chiles, undrained
1 (15-ounce) can tomato sauce
1 (1¼-ounce) mild chili seasoning mix
2 (15-ounce) cans chili beans, drained

In slow cooker, place chicken. In medium bowl, combine tomatoes, tomato sauce, and chili seasoning. Mix well. Cover and cook on low 7 to 9 hours. Stir to break up chicken. Stir in chili beans. Cover and cook 20 minutes. Makes 6 servings.

If thick ketchup won't come out of the bottle, place a drinking straw in the bottle to allow air to flow in, and the ketchup will pour right out.

MEXICAN CHICKEN STEW
(Slow Cooker)

4 chicken breasts, boneless, skinless, cut into cubes
4 medium potatoes, peeled, cubed
1 (15-ounce) can mild salsa
1 (4-ounce) can diced green chiles
1 (1¼-ounce) package taco seasoning mix
1 (8-ounce) can tomato sauce

In slow cooker, combine all ingredients. Mix well. Cover and cook on low 7 to 8 hours. Makes 6 to 8 servings.

HAVING STEW FOR DINNER

2 pounds sirloin, cubed, browned
2 (10¾-ounce) cans mushroom soup
1½ cans milk
4 medium potatoes, sliced
4 carrots, sliced
1 teaspoon salt

Preheat oven to 325 degrees. In large baking dish, combine all ingredients. Cover tightly. Bake 2½ to 3 hours. Do not uncover until end of baking. Makes 6 servings.

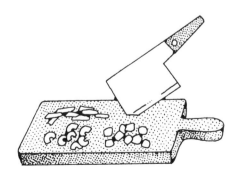

TAKING THE DAY OFF BEEF STEW
(Slow Cooker)

4 medium red potatoes

1½ pounds beef stew meat

⅓ cup flour

1 (14-ounce) can diced tomatoes, undrained

3 cups frozen stir-fry bell pepper and onions

Scrub potatoes and cut each into quarters. In slow cooker, place potatoes. In medium bowl, combine meat and flour, add to slow cooker. Add tomatoes. Mix well. Cover and cook on low 7 to 8 hours. Add stir-fry. Salt and pepper to taste. Cover and cook 40 minutes. Makes 4 to 6 servings.

FARMERS MARKET STEW
(Slow Cooker)

1 pound ground beef, browned

2 cups tomato salsa

2 tablespoons chili powder

1 (15-ounce) can corn, undrained

1 (15-ounce) can green beans undrained

1 (16-ounce) bag stew vegetables

In slow cooker, combine all ingredients. Mix well. Cover and cook on low 7 to 9 hours. Makes 8 to 10 servings.

ALMOST FROM SCRATCH STEW
(Slow Cooker)

5 cups fresh chopped potatoes, carrots, onions, celery
3 cups water
1 (1¼-ounce) package beef stew seasoning
2 pounds stew meat, cut into 1-inch cubes, coat in flour

In slow cooker, combine all ingredients. Mix well. Cover and cook on low 8 to 9 hours. Makes 6 servings.

TACO WITH A TWIST CASSEROLE

1 pound ground beef
1 (1¼-ounce) package taco seasoning mix
1 (15-ounce) can tomato sauce
¼ cup chopped green pepper
1 (8-ounce) package corkscrew macaroni, cooked
1 cup shredded Cheddar cheese
1 cup sour cream

Preheat oven to 350 degrees. In large saucepan, combine beef, taco seasoning, tomato sauce, and green pepper. Cook over medium heat. Bring to a boil. Remove from heat. In medium bowl, combine macaroni, cheese, and sour cream. Mix well. Pour into 2-quart baking dish. Add meat mixture over top. Bake 35 to 40 minutes. Makes 6 to 8 servings.

 To remove moisture or left over scraps from a meat grinder, run several soda crackers through it.

TACO HOT DISH

1½ pounds ground beef
1 (15-ounce) can chili with beans
½ cup taco sauce
½ cup tomato sauce
1 (8-ounce) can enchilada sauce
1½ cups broken taco chips
1 cup shredded Cheddar cheese

Preheat oven to 350 degrees. In large skillet, cook beef until brown, drain. In small bowl, combine taco sauce, tomato sauce, and enchilada sauce. In 2-quart baking dish, layer with chips, beef, and sauce mixture. Bake 25 to 30 minutes. Note: Top with shredded lettuce and shredded cheese (optional). Makes 4 to 6 servings.

TAMALE BAKED PIE

2 cups chili con carne
½ cup chopped onion
7 tamales, cut into 1-inch pieces
2 cups broken corn chips
1 cup grated Cheddar cheese

In 1½-quart baking dish, pour chili. Top with onions, tamales, corn chips, and cheese. Bake 30 minutes. Makes 4 servings.

BEEF ENCHILADAS

1 pound ground beef
1 cup salsa
2 cups shredded Mexican cheese
10 flour tortillas

In large skillet over medium heat, brown beef, drain. Add a ½ cup salsa and ½ cup cheese. Cook until cheese melts. Place tortillas on cookie sheet. Spoon ¼ cup mixture in center of each tortilla. Roll up. Place tortillas seam side down in microwave baking dish. Top with remaining salsa and cheese. Microwave on high until cheese melts. Makes 5 servings.

IN MINUTES ENCHILADAS

10 flour tortillas
1½ cups shredded Cheddar cheese
1 cup diced tomatoes and green chiles
1 (15-ounce) can enchilada sauce
1 cup chopped onion

Sprinkle each tortilla with cheese and 1 tablespoon of tomatoes. Roll tortillas and place seam side down in microwave safe dish. Pour enchilada sauce over tortillas. Cover and cook on high 3 to 5 minutes. Top with onions. Makes 4 to 5 servings.

MEXI BEEF SKILLET

1 pound lean ground beef, cooked, drained
1⅔ cups water
1 (10-ounce) can diced mild tomatoes and green chiles
1 (11-ounce) can Mexicorn, drained
1 (4.4 ounce) package Spanish rice mix
1½ cups shredded Mexican cheese

In large saucepan, combine beef, water, diced tomatoes, corn, and rice mix. Mix well. Cook over medium low heat 15 minutes or until rice is tender. Stir in 1 cup cheese until melted. Sprinkle with remaining half-cup cheese. Makes 5 to 6 servings.

MEXICAN CHICKEN DISH
(Slow Cooker)

5 or 6 skinless, boneless, chicken breasts
1 (15-ounce) can black beans, rinsed, drained
2 (15-ounce) cans corn, drained
1 cup chunky salsa
1 cup Cheddar cheese

In slow cooker, place chicken. In large bowl, combine beans, corn, and salsa, mix well. Pour mixture over chicken. Cover and cook on high 3 hours. Sprinkle cheese over mixture. Cover and cook 10 minutes. Makes 6 to 8 servings.

To make pretty gravy for chicken and noodle dishes, mix in a few drops of yellow food coloring.

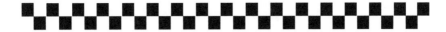

CHICKEN POT PIE

1 (10¾-ounce) can cream of chicken soup

1 cup chopped cooked chicken

1 (10 ounce) package frozen vegetables, thawed

1 cup Bisquick®

½ cup milk

1 egg

Preheat oven to 400 degrees. In medium bowl, combine soup, chicken, and vegetables. Mix well. Pour mixture in 9-inch pie pan. In small bowl, combine Bisquick, milk, and egg. Mix well. Pour over chicken mixture. Bake 30 minutes. Makes 4 servings.

JUST RIGHT CHICKEN POT PIES

1 (10-count) can refrigerated biscuits

1 cup diced cooked chicken

1 (10¾-ounce) can cream of chicken soup

1 cup mixed vegetables from can

Preheat oven to 400 degrees. Separate biscuits and place each biscuit in cup of ungreased muffin pan. Press biscuit up sides to edge of cup. In medium bowl, combine chicken, soup, and mixed vegetables. Mix well. Spoon mixture evenly into cups. Bake 12 to 15 minutes or until golden brown. Makes 5 servings.

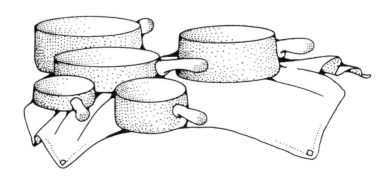

CHICK N BROCCOLI SKILLET

¼ cup Miracle Whip®

2 cups uncooked chicken breast, cubed

1 (10-ounce) package frozen chopped broccoli, thawed, drained

1 cup shredded Velveeta® cheese

In large skillet, combine Miracle Whip and uncooked chicken. Cook over medium low heat 8 minutes, stir often. Add broccoli, cook 5 minutes. Add cheese. Mix well. Cook until hot. Serve over hot rice. Makes 4 servings.

PENNY SAVER CHICKEN DISH
(Slow Cooker)

1 (10¾-ounce) can cream of celery soup

¼ cup milk

2 cups cubed cooked chicken

1 (14.5-ounce) can sliced green beans, drained

In slow cooker, combine all ingredients. Mix Well. Cover and cook on low 4 to 5 hours. Makes 4 servings.

QUICK-N-EASY CHICKEN CASSEROLE

8 cups cubed cooked chicken
2 (10¾-ounce) cans cream of chicken soup
1 cup sour cream
25 butter flavored crackers, crushed
2 tablespoons butter or margarine, melted
1 teaspoons celery seed

In large bowl, combine chicken, soup, and sour cream. Spread mixture into 13 x 9-inch baking dish. In small bowl, combine cracker crumbs, butter, and celery seeds. Mix well. Sprinkle over chicken mixture. Bake 30 to 35 minutes. Makes 8 to 10 servings.

EVERYONE'S FAVORITE CHICKEN CASSEROLE
(Busy Women's Cookbook)

2½ or 3 pounds chicken, cooked
2 (6-ounce) boxes Pepperidge Farm® 1 Step Stuffing
1½ (10 ¾-ounce) cans cream of chicken soup
1½ cups plain yogurt

Preheat oven to 350 degrees. Pull cooked chicken from bone, set aside. Fix stuffing according to directions on box. Spread half of stuffing in 2-quart baking dish. Cover stuffing with chicken. Spread soup and yogurt over chicken and sprinkle with rest of stuffing. Bake for 55 to 60 minutes. Makes 6 servings.

 To cut the acidity level of tomato-based sauces and stews, such as chili or spaghetti sauce, add a pinch of baking soda while cooking.

WILD STUFFING AROUND TURKEY
(Slow Cooker)

4 to 5 pounds boneless whole turkey breast
4 cups cooked wild rice
1 small onion, chopped
½ cup dried cranberries
2 apples, peeled chopped

In slow cooker, place turkey. In large bowl, combine rice, onion, cranberries, and apples. Mix well. Spoon mixture around turkey, push mixture down lightly around turkey. Cover and cook on low 9 to 10 hours. Makes 6 to 8 servings.

FROM THE PAST CASSEROLE

1 pound sausage
2 medium onions, sliced
4 medium potatoes, sliced
½ teaspoon salt
1 (15-ounce) can cream style corn
1 (8-ounce) can tomato sauce

Preheat oven to 350 degrees. Shape sausage into 18, 1½-inch meatballs. Spray 2-quart baking dish with cooking spray. Place onions and potatoes in baking dish, sprinkle salt over potatoes. Add corn and meatballs. Pour tomato sauce over mixture. Cover and bake 30 minutes. Uncover, bake for 45 minutes. Makes 6 servings.

MEAL IN A CASSEROLE

1½ pounds lean ground beef, browned, drained
1 cup shredded Cheddar cheese
1 (15-ounce) can corn, drained
3 cups cooked macaroni and cheese

Preheat oven 350 degrees. In 2-quart baking dish, add beef. Sprinkle cheese over top. Spoon corn and macaroni evenly over mixture. Bake 40 to 50 minutes. Makes 6 servings.

5 LAYER HAMBURGER CASSEROLE

1 pound ground beef, browned, drained
1 (15-ounce) can French style green beans, drained
1½ cups shredded mozzarella cheese
1 (10¾-ounce) can of mushroom soup
4 cups tator tots

Preheat oven to 350 degrees. In 1½-quart baking dish, layer hamburger, green beans, mozzarella cheese, and mushroom soup. Bake 1 hour. Top mixture with tator tots. Bake 30 minutes Makes 6 to 8 servings.

CORNED BEEF AND CABBAGE
(Slow Cooker)

3 carrots, cut in 3 inch pieces
1 (3 to 4 pound) corned beef brisket
2 onions, quartered
1 medium cabbage, cut in wedges
2 cups water

In slow cooker, add carrots, brisket, onion, cabbage, and water. Cover and cook on low 10 to 12 hours. After 6 to 8 hours, push cabbage wedges down into liquid. Makes 6 servings.

POTATOES UNDER BEEF ROAST
(Slow Cooker)

4 medium potatoes, sliced
2½ to 3 pounds chuck roast, browned
2 (10¾-ounce) cans of mushroom soup
1 soup can water
½ soup can evaporated milk

In slow cooker, place potatoes. Add roast. In small bowl, combine soups, water, and evaporated milk. Mix well. Pour mixture over roast. Cover and cook on low 8 to 10 hours. Makes 4 to 6 servings.

CHICKEN STIR FRY

¾ cup Catalina dressing
¼ cup soy sauce
½ teaspoon garlic powder
2 cups cubed cooked chicken breast
1 (16-ounce) package frozen mixed vegetables, thawed

In large skillet, combine all ingredients. Mix well. Cook over medium heat, stirring occasionally until hot. Serve with hot rice. Makes 4 servings.

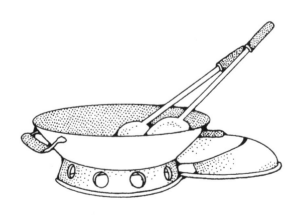

AFTER WORK STIR FRY

3 cups frozen mixed vegetables
1 tablespoon oil
1 (6-ounce) package grilled chicken breast strips
½ cup sweet 'n sour sauce
1 boil-in-bag, white rice, prepared

In medium skillet with oil, add vegetables, cook over medium heat 5 minutes or until vegetables are tender. Add chicken and sauce. Cover and cook 2 minutes or until mixture is hot. Makes 2 or 3 servings.

AFTER A LONG DAY STIR FRY

1 (12-ounce) package frozen breaded cooked chicken
   nuggets
1 (1 pound .5-ounce) Create a Meal® frozen Sweet &
   Sour Stir Fry Meal Starter
3 cups cooked instant white rice

Cook chicken as directed on package. In large skillet, combine frozen vegetables and contents of stir fry meal starter. Mix well. Cover and cook over medium heat 7 to 10 minutes, or until vegetables are crisp-tender, stirring frequently. Add chicken. Mix well. Serve over hot rice. Makes 3 servings.

HOT OFF THE STOVE STROGANOFF

1 pound ground beef, browned
1 cup sour cream
1 (4-ounce) jar mushrooms, drained
¼ cup ketchup

In medium saucepan, combine all ingredients. Mix well. Cook over low heat 15 minute, stirring occasionally. Serve over noodles. Makes 4 servings.

LEFT OVER CHICKEN SANDWICHES

2 cups cubed cooked chicken

1 stalk celery, chopped

⅓ cup mayonnaise

1 cup cubed American cheese

6 buns

Preheat oven to 450 degrees. In cooking sprayed 1½-quart baking dish, combine all ingredients. Mix well. Cover and bake 35 to 40 minutes, stirring occasionally. Makes 6 servings.

CREAMY & HOT CHICKEN WRAPS

2 cups chicken, cooked and diced

1 large stalk celery, diced

1 tablespoon diced onion

1 cup shredded Cheddar cheese

½ cup Miracle Whip®

buns

Preheat oven to 325 degrees. In medium bowl, combine all ingredients. Mix well. Place a scoop of mixture on each bun. Wrap in foil. Bake 35 to 40 minutes. Makes 4 servings.

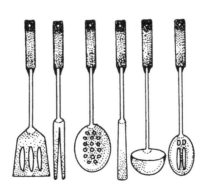

ITALIAN MEATBALL SUBS
(Slow Cooker)

10 (1- to 1½-inch) frozen cooked Italian meatballs
1½ cups sliced fresh mushrooms
¼ cup chopped green pepper
1 small onion, sliced
1½ cups pasta sauce
½ cup shredded mozzarella cheese
2 hoagie buns, split, toasted

In slow cooker, combine meatballs, mushrooms, green pepper, onion, and tomato pasta sauce. Mix well. Cover and cook on low 8 to 9 hours. Place mixture on buns. Sprinkle cheese on top. Makes 2 subs. Can double recipe.

TUNA MELTS

1 (12-ounce) can chunk white tuna, drained
1½ cups coleslaw mix
3 tablespoons mayonnaise
1 tablespoon Dijon mustard
4 English muffins, split and lightly toasted
½ cup shredded Cheddar cheese

Preheat broiler. In medium bowl, combine tuna and coleslaw. In small bowl, combine mayonnaise and mustard. Mix well. Spread tuna mixture onto muffin halves. Sprinkle cheese on top. Broil 4 inches from heat 2 to 3 minutes. Makes 4 servings.

EASY-DOES-IT DUMPLINGS

1¼ cups flour
2 teaspoons baking powder
1 teaspoon salt
1 egg, beaten
⅔ to ¾ cup milk

In medium bowl, combine flour, baking powder, and salt. Mix well. Beat in egg and milk. Drop by teaspoonfuls in simmering stew or liquid. Cook 10 to 12 minutes. Makes 6 servings.

RISE & SHINE CASSEROLE

¼ cup oil
2 cups frozen hash browns
1 cup chopped ham
½ cup chopped onion
6 eggs
1 cup shredded Cheddar cheese

In large skillet with oil, add hash browns, ham, and onions, cook over medium heat 8 to 10 minutes. Add eggs and cheese, cook until eggs are set. Stir often. Makes 4 servings.

 For ready-to-eat bacon, cook the entire package, drain it, place it in plastic freezer bags, and freeze. Remove the slices you need and reheat in the microwave.

EARLY RISER CASSEROLE

4 slices bread
1 pound sausage, cooked, drained
2 cups shredded Cheddar cheese
6 eggs, beaten
2 cups milk
1 teaspoon dry mustard

Preheat oven to 350 degrees. Spray bottom of 2-quart baking dish with cooking spray. Tear up 4 slices of bread and place in bottom of dish. Sprinkle sausage and cheese over bread. In small bowl, combine eggs, milk, and mustard. Mix well. Pour over sausage mixture. Bake 35 to 40 minutes. Makes 6 servings.

NO KIDDING PINEAPPLE STUFFING
(Slow Cooker)

1 (20-ounce) can crushed pineapple, undrained
¼ cup evaporated milk
1 cup packaged cornbread crumbs
½ cup sugar
¼ cup melted butter or margarine
3 eggs

In slow cooker, spray with cooking spray. In large bowl, combine all ingredients. Mix well. Pour mixture in slow cooker. Cover. Cook on high 2½ to 3 hours. Makes 4 to 6 servings.

NOTE: Good with ham.

POUR SAUCE OVER VEGETABLES

2 tablespoons butter or margarine
2 tablespoons all purpose flour
¼ teaspoon salt
1 cup milk
1 cup shredded Cheddar cheese

In small saucepan, melt butter. Stir in flour and salt. Add milk. Cook and stir over medium heat until thickened and bubbly. Cook 1 to 2 minutes more. Remove from heat. Add cheese. Blend until cheese melts. Spoon over cooked vegetables. Makes 1¼ cups.

CHEDDAR CHEESE POTATO TOPPER

1 (10¾-ounce) can Cheddar cheese soup
⅓ cup milk
½ cup sour cream

In small saucepan, combine all ingredients. Mix well. Cook over medium heat until hot. Serve over baked potatoes. Makes 4 servings.

BROCCOLI CHEESE POTATO TOPPER

1 (10¾-ounce) can Cheddar cheese soup
2 tablespoons sour cream
½ teaspoon Dijon mustard
1 cup cooked broccoli

In medium saucepan, combine soup, sour cream, and mustard. Mix well. Cook over medium heat until hot. Add broccoli, cook 1 minute. Pour mixture over baked potato. Makes 4 servings.

MOCK HOLLANDAISE SAUCE

¼ cup sour cream

¼ cup Miracle Whip®

1 teaspoon lemon juice

½ teaspoon mustard

In small saucepan, combine all ingredients. Cook and stir over medium heat until heated through (do not boil). Serve with vegetables.

NOTES

BREADS

INVENTIONS AND FACTS

1. Wonder Bread® popularized pre-sliced bread in 1930.

2. The modern timer, pop-up toaster was invented by Charles Strite in 1919.

3. The toaster was actually invented before sliced bread.

4. After 16 years of working on it, Otto Fredrick Rohwedder designed a machine in 1928 that sliced bread and wrapped it.

5. Mayonnaise was invented in France in 1756, but was first mass marketed as "Hellman's Blue Ribbon Mayonnaise" in 1912.

6. Olemargarine was patented by Henry W. Bradley of Binghamton, NY, in 1871.

7. In the 1700's John Montagu the 4th Earl of Sandwich, originated the sandwich (meat between slices of bread) so he could have a hand free to play cards.

8. Dr Percy Spencer, an engineer at Raytheon Corporation, is probably the father of microwave cooking, learned from experiments in 1946.

EXTRA FLAVOR CHEESE BREAD

2 cups shredded Cheddar cheese
½ cup mayonnaise
2 tablespoons diced pimientos
1 pound loaf sourdough French bread

In medium bowl, combine cheese, mayonnaise and pimientos. Mix well. Cut bread loaf in half lengthwise. Place cut side up on broiler pan. Broil 6 to 8 inches from heat, until lightly toasted. Remove bread. Spread mixture on top. Return to broiler. Broil 2 to 3 minutes or until cheese mixture bubbles and begins to brown. Makes 12 to 16 servings.

MARMALADE BREAD

1 loaf French bread
½ cup butter or margarine
½ cup orange marmalade
3 tablespoons cinnamon

Preheat oven to 400 degrees. Cut bread into 1½-inch diagonal slices. Spread butter and marmalade. Sprinkle cinnamon over top. Place slices on ungreased baking sheet. Bake 8 to 10 minutes. Makes 8 to 10 slices.

CHEESY SNACK BREAD

1 pound loaf frozen white bread, thawed
2 tablespoons butter, melted
2 cups shredded Monterey Jack cheese
¼ cup diced green onions
½ cup real bacon bits

Preheat oven to 375 degrees. Press dough into greased baking sheet. Drizzle butter over top. Sprinkle cheese, green onions, and bacon bits over bread. Bake 15 to 20 minutes. Makes 20 servings.

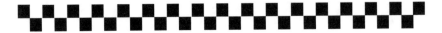

SOBER BREAD

3 cups self-rising flour

2 tablespoons sugar

1 (12-ounce) can beer

3 tablespoons butter, melted

Preheat oven to 350 degrees. In large bowl, combine flour, sugar, and beer. Mix well. Pour mixture into greased loaf pan. Bake 55 to 60 minutes. Brush top of loaf with butter.

LITTLE ITALY LOAF

1 (16-ounce) loaf frozen bread dough, thawed

3 tablespoons butter, softened

2 tablespoons dry spaghetti sauce mix

2 tablespoons Parmesan cheese

Preheat oven to 350 degrees. On a floured surface, roll dough to 12 x 9-inch rectangle. In small bowl, combine remaining ingredients, mix well. Spread over dough. Roll up jelly roll style, seal edges. Place seam down on a greased baking sheet. Slash top at 2-inch intervals. Let rise in warm place 30 minutes or until doubled. Bake 30 minutes, cover with foil, bake an additional 15 minutes.

BACON BREAD

1 (1-pound) frozen bread dough, thawed
2 tablespoons vegetable oil, divided
12 bacon strips, cooked and diced
1 cup shredded mozzarella cheese
1 (1-ounce) package ranch salad dressing

Preheat oven to 350 degrees. Roll out dough to ½-inch thickness. Brush with 1 tablespoon oil. Cut into 1 inch pieces, place in large bowl. Add remaining ingredients, toss well. Arrange in greased 9 x 5-inch oval baking pan. Cover, let rise in warm place for 30 minutes or until double. Bake 15 minutes. Cover with foil, bake 10 minutes or until golden brown.

BASIC YEAST BREAD

1 cup milk
1 teaspoon salt
1 egg
2 tablespoons butter, softened
3¼ cups all-purpose flour
1 tablespoon sugar
2 teaspoon active dry yeast

Place all ingredients in bread machine pan in order specified by owner's manual. Program dough cycle setting. Press start. Makes 1 loaf

 Freshen slightly stale bread, doughnuts, or biscuits, by placing them in a wide mouth jar with a damp paper towel. Close the lid and leave overnight.

PARMESAN SLICES

¼ cup butter or margarine, melted
½ cup grated Parmesan cheese
6 (1-inch) slices Vienna bread

In small bowl, combine butter and cheese. Brush mixture on bread slices. Place slices on baking sheet. Broil until lightly brown. Makes 6 servings.

ITALIAN BREAD SLICES

¾ cup butter, softened
2 tablespoons garlic powder
1 cup grated fresh Parmesan cheese
1 loaf Italian bread

Preheat oven to 350 degrees. In small bowl, combine butter, garlic, and Parmesan cheese. Cut bread in 1-inch slices. Spread mixture over bread slices. Place slices on baking sheet. Bake 8 to 10 minutes. Makes 8 to 10 servings.

ONE SLICE GRILLED CHEESE

4 slices toast, lightly browned
4 teaspoons butter or margarine
4 slices American cheese

On cooking sheet, place toast. Spread butter over top. Place 1 slice cheese on each slice. Broil until cheese melts. Note: Great with soup. Makes 4 servings.

TOASTED BREAD SLICES

3 tablespoons butter
½ cup diced onions
1 teaspoon diced garlic
1 loaf French bread
1½ cups shredded Swiss cheese

In small bowl, combine butter, onions, and garlic. Mix well. Cut bread in 1-inch slices. Spread mixture over bread. Sprinkle cheese on top. Place on baking sheet. Broil until cheese melts.

SKILLET FRIED BREAD

½ cup butter or margarine, softened
2 cloves garlic, minced
1 loaf French bread, cut into 1-inch slices

In small bowl, combine butter and garlic. Mix well. Spread mixture on both sides of bread. In large skillet, brown on both sides, over medium high heat.

LITTLE HOT BISCUITS

2 cups Bisquick®
1 cup grated Cheddar cheese
¼ teaspoon red pepper
1 cup milk

Preheat oven to 450 degrees. In medium bowl, combine all ingredients. Mix well. Drop mixture by tablespoon onto lightly greased baking sheet. Bake 15 minutes or until golden brown. Makes 9 biscuits.

HAM DROP BISCUITS

1 cup milk
2 cups Bisquick®
¼ cup shredded Cheddar cheese
⅓ cup diced ham

Preheat oven to 400 degrees. In medium bowl, combine all ingredients. Mix well. Drop mixture by tablespoon on baking sheet. Bake 12 to 15 minutes. Makes 12 biscuits.

MAYONNAISE BISCUITS

2 cups self–rising flour
1 cup milk
4 tablespoons mayonnaise

Preheat oven to 400 degrees. In medium bowl, combine all ingredients, forming stiff dough. Drop mixture by tablespoon into greased muffin pan. Bake 12 to 15 minutes. Makes 12.

PULL APART PARMESAN BISCUITS

3 tablespoons butter or margarine, melted
2 tablespoons finely chopped onion
1 teaspoon Italian seasoning
1 (12-ounce) package refrigerated buttermilk biscuits
¼ cup Parmesan cheese

Preheat oven to 400 degrees. In 9-inch round cake pan. pour butter, coat bottom evenly. Sprinkle onion and seasoning in bottom of pan. Cut each biscuit in half. In small bowl, place cheese. Coat all sides of biscuit pieces with cheese. Arrange single layer in pan, sprinkle remaining cheese over top. Bake 15 minutes or until golden brown.

RESTAURANT CHEESE BISCUITS

2 cups Bisquick®
²⁄₃ cup milk
½ cup shredded Cheddar cheese
¼ cup butter or margarine, melted
¼ teaspoon garlic powder

Preheat oven to 450 degrees. In medium bowl, combine Bisquik, milk, and cheese, stir until moistened. Drop by tablespoon onto greased cookie sheet, 2-inches apart. In small bowl, combine butter and garlic. Lightly brush top of each biscuit, set remaining butter aside. Bake 10 minutes or until golden brown. Top with remaining butter mixture.

KOOKY COCONUT DROP BISCUITS

2 cups Bisquick®
¾ cup toasted coconut flakes
2 tablespoons sugar
⅓ cup vegetable shortening
1 cup milk
½ teaspoon vanilla

Preheat oven to 450 degrees. In a large bowl combine Bisquick, coconut, and sugar. Cut in shortening, until coarse crumbs. In a small bowl, combine milk and vanilla. Make a well in center of dry mixture. Stir till just mixed, do not over mix. Drop by tablespoon onto greased baking sheet. Bake 10 to 12 minutes. Makes 12 to 15 biscuits.

 To keep rolls warm longer, place a piece of aluminum foil under a cloth napkin in the bottom of the serving basket.

TOSS AND ROLL BISCUITS

1 (10 count) can biscuits
3 tablespoons butter or margarine
½ teaspoon chili powder
½ cup shredded Cheddar cheese
¼ cup chopped jalapeno peppers

Preheat oven to 375 degrees. Cut biscuits into quarters. In 9-inch pie pan, combine butter and chili. Mix well. Place biscuits pieces in pie pan and toss to coat each piece in mixture. Sprinkle cheese and peppers on top. Bake 12 to 15 minutes.

CINNAMON BAKED BISCUITS

1 (10 count) can refrigerated biscuits
⅓ cup butter or margarine
¼ cup sugar
2 tablespoons brown sugar
1 teaspoon cinnamon

Preheat oven to 400 degrees. Place biscuits on baking sheet. In small bowl, combine butter, sugar, brown sugar, and cinnamon. Mix well. Spread mixture over biscuits. Bake 8 to 10 minutes. Makes 10 biscuits.

TENDER LAYER BISCUITS

1 (10 count) can tender layers biscuits
10 slices bacon, browned crisp, crumbled
2 tablespoons butter or margarine

Preheat oven to 400 degrees. Place biscuits on baking sheet. Pull half of layers off biscuits. Put 1 slice of crumbled bacon on each biscuit. Put layers back on biscuits. Brush butter on top of each biscuit. Bake 8 to 10 minutes. Makes 10 biscuits.

WRAP BAKED ROLLS

1 cup whipped cream cheese with pimientos
1 teaspoon garlic powder
1 teaspoon diced green onions
8 to 10 hard rolls

Preheat oven to 375 degrees. In small bowl, combine cream cheese, garlic powder, and green onions. Mix well. Split rolls lengthwise, but not through. Spread mixture on roll. Wrap roll in heavy duty foil. Bake15 minutes. Makes 8 to 10 servings.

CHEESY BROWN 'N SERVE ROLLS
(Homemade Blessings)

¼ cup butter, softened
¼ cup mayonnaise
¼ cup Parmesan cheese
1 dozen brown and serve rolls

Preheat oven to 350 degrees. In small bowl, combine butter, mayonnaise, and cheese. Mix well. Place rolls on ungreased baking sheet. Brush tops with cheese mixture. Bake 15 minutes or until golden brown. Makes 12 rolls.

FLIP FLOP NUT ROLLS

½ cup chocolate syrup
2 tablespoons butter, melted
½ cup chopped pecans
1 (8 ounce) can refrigerated breadsticks

Preheat oven to 350 degrees. In 9-inch round cake pan, combine syrup and butter. Sprinkle nuts over mixture. Separate, but do not uncoil breadsticks. Arrange dough coils over nuts. Bake for 20 to 25 minutes or until golden brown. Flip pan upside down on serving plate. Let stand 2 minutes. Remove pan.

SWEET CRESCENT ROLLS

1 (8 count) can crescent rolls
1 cup confectioners sugar
1½ cups apple pie filling

Unroll crescent rolls. Place on baking sheet. Sprinkle 2 tablespoons sugar over rolls. Top with 2 tablespoons apple pie filling in center of each roll. Roll up dough. Bake according to directions on can. Sprinkle with sugar. Makes 4 to 6 servings.

QUICK POPPY SEED ROLLS

1 (8-ounce) package brown and serve rolls
2½ tablespoons butter or margarine, melted
¼ teaspoon garlic powder
1 teaspoon poppy seeds

Place rolls on ungreased baking sheet. Brush top of rolls with butter. Sprinkle garlic powder and poppy seeds on top. Bake as directed on package.

HUSH PUPPIES

1 cup yellow cornmeal
¾ teaspoon baking powder
½ cup milk
1 egg
¼ cup diced onions
Oil

In medium bowl, combine cornmeal and baking powder. Mix well. Add milk, egg, and onions. Mix well. Drop batter by teaspoons in skillet with hot oil. Cook 3 to 5 minutes or until golden brown. Drain on paper towel. Makes 4 to 6 servings.

GOLDEN HUSH PUPPIES

2½ cups self-rising cornmeal

3 tablespoons self-rising flour

2 eggs

½ cup milk

¼ cup diced onions

Oil

In large bowl, combine all ingredients. Drop mixture by tablespoon in skillet with hot oil. Cook until golden brown. Makes 4 to 6 servings.

FRIED CORNBREAD

1½ cups self-rising cornmeal

1 egg

1½ cups milk

oil

In large bowl, combine all ingredients. Mix well. Drop mixture by tablespoon in hot skillet with oil. Cook until golden brown on both sides. Makes 4 to6 servings.

SKILLET FRIED CORNBREAD

1 cup cornmeal

½ teaspoon baking soda

1 teaspoon salt

1 egg, beaten

1¼ cups buttermilk

oil

In large bowl, combine all ingredients, except oil. Beat until smooth. Pour 1 tablespoon of batter in hot skillet with little oil. Cook until brown on both sides. Makes 6 servings.

CREAM-STYLE CORN BREAD

1 cup self-rising cornmeal

2 eggs

1 cup cream-style corn

1 cup sour cream

Preheat oven to 400 degrees. In medium bowl, combine all ingredients. Mix well. Pour mixture into 1½-quart baking dish sprayed with cooking spray. Bake 30 to 40 minutes. Makes 4 to 6 servings.

MEXICAN CORNBREAD

1 egg

1¼ cups milk

3 tablespoons butter or margarine

1½ cups self-rising cornmeal

½ cup shredded Cheddar cheese

3 tablespoons diced jalapeno peppers

Preheat oven to 400 degrees. In large bowl, combine all ingredients. Mix well. Pour mixture into 9-inch baking dish. Bake 25 to 30 minutes.

MORE THAN CORNBREAD

1 (12-ounce) package corn muffin mix

1 cup niblets corn

¼ cup diced onion

1 egg, beaten

⅔ cup milk

Preheat oven to 400 degrees. In large bowl, combine muffin mix, corn, onion, egg, and milk. Blend until mixed. Spread mixture in cooking sprayed 8 x 8-inch baking pan. Bake 20 to 25 minutes. Makes 6 to 8 servings.

CORNBREAD JOHNNY CAKE

1 Jiffy® corn muffin mix
1 egg
⅓ cup milk
1 tablespoon butter, melted

Preheat oven to 400 degrees. In medium bowl, combine all ingredients. Mix well. Pour mixture into greased 8 x 8-inch square baking pan. Bake 20 to 25 minutes.

SKILLET CORNBREAD

2 eggs
1 tablespoon sugar
½ cup butter or margarine, melted
1½ cups milk
1½ cups self-rising cornmeal

Preheat oven to 400 degrees. In medium iron skillet, grease with butter. In large bowl, combine all ingredients. Mix well. Pour mixture in skillet. Bake 30 minutes or until golden brown. Makes 6 servings.

EASY TO FIX BANANA BREAD

2 cups mashed ripe bananas
1 teaspoon vanilla
3 eggs
2 cups Bisquick®
1 cup sugar

Preheat oven to 350 degrees. In large bowl, combine all ingredients. Mix well. Pour mixture into greased 9 x 5 x 3-inch loaf pan. Bake 55 to 60 minutes. Cool before serving.

GOING BANANAS BREAD

2½ cups flour
1 cup brown sugar
3½ teaspoons baking powder
2 or 3 ripe bananas
⅓ cup milk
3 tablespoons vegetable oil

Preheat oven to 350 degrees. In a large bowl, combine flour, brown sugar, baking powder. Add remaining ingredients. Mix well with an electric mixer. Grease only the bottom of two loaf pans, pour in batter. Bake 55 minutes.

CORN MUFFINS SURPRISE

1 (8½-ounce) package muffin mix
1 (7-ounce) can niblets corn, drained
¼ teaspoon cinnamon
¼ cup chopped walnuts

Preheat oven to 400 degrees. In medium bowl, prepare corn muffins as directed on package. Add corn, cinnamon, and walnuts. Mix well. Spray 8 muffin cups with non-stick cooking spray. Pour batter evenly among muffin cups. Bake 15 to 20 minutes. Makes 8 muffins

LEMON SURPREME MUFFINS

1 box lemon supreme cake mix
1 (4-serving) box instant lemon pudding
½ cup oil
1 cup buttermilk
4 eggs, beaten

Preheat oven to 375 degrees. In large bowl, combine all ingredients. Mix well. Pour mixture in muffin pan with paper liners three-fourths full. Bake 15 to 20 minutes.

STUFFED CRUST FOR PIZZA

1 (10-ounce) can pizza crust
7 pieces string cheese

Preheat oven to 425 degrees. Spray 13 x 9-inch baking pan. unroll dough and press in bottom and up one inch on sides of pan. Place pieces of cheese along edges. Fold dough over cheese. Press edge to seal. Top with your favorite toppings. Bake 15 to 18 minutes. Makes 1 pizza.

PARMESAN BREADSTICKS

1 (11-ounce) can soft breadsticks, cut in half to make 16 breadsticks
3 tablespoons butter or margarine, melted
¾ cup grated Parmesan cheese

Preheat oven to 350 degrees. Twist and shape dough to make 16 breadsticks. Brush butter over top. Sprinkle cheese on top. Bake 12 to 15 minutes until golden brown. Makes 16 breadsticks.

PIZZA BREAD STICKS

1 (8-ounce) package pepperoni

1 (10.6-ounce) package refrigerated Parmesan and garlic breadsticks

1½ cups finely shredded mozzarella cheese

1 cup warm pizza sauce

Preheat oven to 375 degrees. On baking sheets, place breadsticks in single layer. Top each with 5 slices pepperoni and sprinkle cheese on top. Bake for 10 to 12 minutes. Serve breadsticks with warm pizza sauce. Makes 20 breadsticks.

OPEN SESAME BREAD TWIST

1 (11-ounce) package refrigerated breadsticks

1 egg white, slightly beaten

1¼ teaspoons sesame seeds

1 teaspoon garlic salt

Preheat oven to 375 degrees. Prepare breadsticks according to package instructions. Brush tops with egg white. Sprinkle with sesame seeds and garlic salt. Bake 13 minutes or until golden brown. Makes 12 breadsticks.

BAKED PITA WEDGES

½ cup mayonnaise

¼ cup diced green onions

1 (8-ounce) package shredded cheddar cheese

1 (2-ounce) jar diced pimientos, drained

4 (7-inch) pita breads

Preheat oven to 350 degrees. In medium bowl, combine mayonnaise, green onion, cheese, and pimientos. Mix well. Cut each pita bread into 6 wedges. Place on baking sheet. Bake 6 to 7 minutes. Spread mixture on wedges. Bake 6 to 8 minutes. Makes 12 servings.

EASY PANCAKES

2 cups Bisquick®
1½ cups milk
1 tablespoon butter or margarine
2 eggs
1 teaspoon baking powder

In medium bowl, combine all ingredients. Mix well. Pour ¼ cup mixture on hot greased griddle skillet. Cook until brown on both sides. Makes 12 to 14 pancakes.

SOUTHWEST BUTTER

1 cup butter, softened
2 tablespoons salsa
1 tablespoon chopped cilantro

In small bowl, combine all ingredients. Mix well. Use on cornbread, breadsticks, etc.

ITALIAN BUTTER

½ cup butter, softened
1 tablespoon pesto
1 tablespoon Parmesan cheese

In small bowl, combine all ingredients. Mix well. Use for cooking or on bread.

CINNAMON BUTTER

½ cup butter, softened
1 tablespoon packed brown sugar
½ teaspoon sugar
½ teaspoon ground cinnamon

In small bowl, combine all ingredients. Mix well. Use on toast or muffins.

STRAWBERRIES FOR JAM

3 cups large strawberries
3 cups sugar

Wash strawberries and hull. In large saucepan, crush berries and cook over medium low heat until pulp begins to boil. Add sugar. Cook and stir until mixture thickens. Pour into sterilized jars and seal. Makes 3 (6-ounce) jars.

PEACH TREE PRESERVES

2 pounds peaches
3 cups sugar
2 cups water

Remove skin from peaches. Cut in half and remove stones. In large saucepan, boil sugar and water until syrup coat spoon. Add peaches and boil until syrup is thick. Mash. Pour into sterilized jars and seal. Makes 3½ pints.

MAPLE PANCAKE SYRUP

2 cups packed brown sugar
1 cup water
1 tablespoon butter
½ teaspoon maple flavoring

In small saucepan, combine all ingredients. Mix well. Bring to a full boil. Stirring constantly for 2 to 3 minutes. Use on pancakes or French toast.

NOTES

DESSERTS

INVENTIONS AND FACTS

1. The first popsicle was accidentally made by 11 year old Frank Epperson in 1905.

2. Ruth Wakerfield made the first chocolate chip cookies at the Toll House Inn in Whitman, Massachusetts, in 1930.

3. Rufus M. Eastman received the first patent for an electric mixer in 1885.

4. Cotton candy was invented in 1897 by William Morrison and John C. Wharton, candy makers from Nashville, Tennessee.

5. In Cincinnati, Ohio, Willie Johnson, an African American, patented a mechanical egg beater in 1884.

6. Ancient Egyptians were the first to enjoy a gooey treat now called marshmallow as early as 2,000 B.C. The treat was considered very special and was reserved for gods and royalty.

7. Earnest Hamwi popularized the ice cream cone at the 1904 St. Louis World's Fair, but Italo Marchiony had received a patent to manufacture them earlier that year.

8. By 1975 sales of microwave ovens exceeded sales of gas ranges.

HOT FUDGE PIE

1 (1-ounce) unsweetened baking chocolate
8 tablespoons margarine
2 eggs
1 cup sugar
½ cup all-purpose flour
1 teaspoon vanilla

Preheat oven to 350 degrees. In medium saucepan, combine chocolate and margarine. Melt over low heat. In medium bowl, cream eggs and sugar. Add chocolate mixture. Add flour and vanilla. Beat well. Pour into greased 8-inch pie pan. Bake 30 minutes. Cool. Serve with ice cream.

CHOCOLATE PIE

2 (4-serving) packages instant chocolate pudding mix
2 cups cold milk
1 (8-ounce) tub whipped topping, thawed
1 (9-inch) prepared graham cracker pie crust

In large bowl, combine pudding mix and milk. Mix until thickened. Fold in half of whipped topping. Pour into pie crust. Top with remaining whipped topping. Cover and chill 4 hours.

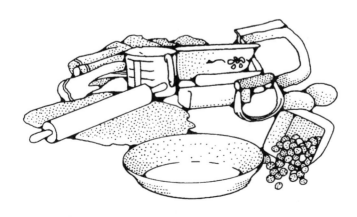

FRENCH SILK PIE

1 cup sugar
¾ cup butter
3 squares baking chocolate, melted
3 eggs
1½ teaspoons vanilla
whipped topping
1 (9-inch) pie crust, baked

In medium bowl, cream sugar and butter. Add chocolate and vanilla. Add eggs one at a time, mixing with electric mixer on medium speed for 2 minutes after each addition. Pour into pie crust. Cover and chill 2 hours. Garnish with whipped topping and optional chocolate curls.

MINT PIE

1 (14-ounce) can sweetened condensed milk
1½ teaspoons peppermint extract
10 drops green food coloring
2 cups whipped topping
1 (6-ounce) prepared chocolate cookie pie crust

In large bowl, combine milk, peppermint extract, and food coloring. Fold in whipped topping. Pour into pie crust. Freeze 6 hours. Freeze leftovers.

To keep brown sugar from lumping, remove it from the original container and store in a tightly sealed glass jar.

LITTLE BIT OF GUILT STRAWBERRY PIE

2 cups vanilla yogurt
1 (8-ounce) tub whipped topping, thawed
2 cups sweetened diced strawberries
1 (9-inch) pie shell, baked

In large bowl, fold yogurt and whipped topping until well blended. Fold in strawberries. Spoon mixture into pie shell. Freeze until firm. Remove from freezer, let set 30 minutes before serving. Makes 6 to 8 servings.

STRAWBERRY CREAM CHEESE PIE

1 (10-ounce) package strawberries halved in syrup
2 (8-ounce) packages cream cheese
¼ cup sugar
1 teaspoon vanilla
2 cups whipped topping
1 (9-inch) chocolate crumb crust

Drain strawberries, reserving ¼ cup liquid. In large bowl, combine strawberries, liquid, cream cheese, sugar, and vanilla. Beat until smooth. Fold in whipped topping. Spoon into crust. Chill several hours. Makes 6 to 8 servings.

IS THIS LEMON PIE?

Frozen or homemade waffles
Confectioners sugar
Fresh lemon juice

Toast waffles, place on plate. Generously sprinkle sugar on waffles. Drizzle fresh lemon juice over sugar.

LEMONADE STAND PIE

1 (6-ounce) can frozen lemonade, partially thawed
2 cups vanilla ice cream, softened
1 (8-ounce) tub whipped topping, thawed
1 (8-inch) graham cracker crumb crust

In large bowl, beat lemonade with electric mixer on low speed 30 seconds. Gradually spoon in ice cream. Beat until well blended. Stir in whipped topping until smooth. Spoon mixture into crust. Freeze. Let stand at room temperature 30 minutes before serving. Makes 6 to 8 servings.

VANILLA TOFFEE CHEESECAKE PIE

1 cup vanilla chips
2 (8-ounce) packages cream cheese, softened
1 (8-ounce) tub frozen whipped topping, thawed
⅓ cup English toffee bits
1 (9-inch) graham cracker crust

In a large saucepan, melt chips over medium low heat. Remove from heat. Add cream cheese, stir until smooth. Fold in whipped topping. Pour into crust. Refrigerate until set. Sprinkle with toffee bits before serving. Makes 6 to 8 servings.

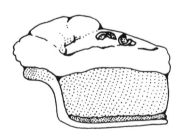

PUMPKIN CREAM PIE

2 cups cold milk

2 (4 serving) boxes instant vanilla pudding and pie filling

1 cup canned pumpkin

1 teaspoon pumpkin pie spice

1 cup whipped topping

1 (9-inch) pie shell, baked

In large bowl, combine milk, pudding, pumpkin, pie spice, and whipped topping. Beat at low speed with electric mixer 1 minute. Pour mixture in pie shell. Chill until set. Garnish with whipped topping.

CREAMY BANANA PIE

2 bananas

2 (4-serving) boxes instant banana pudding and
    pie filling

2½ cups cold milk

2 cups whipped topping

1 (9-inch) pie shell, baked

Slice 1 banana in baked pie shell. Prepare pie filling as directed on package using 2½ cups milk. Fold in ½ cup of whipped topping. Pour mixture over banana in pie shell. Chill until set. Top with remaining whipped topping, garnish with sliced bananas.

For perfect whipped cream, chill cream, beater and bowl before whipping.

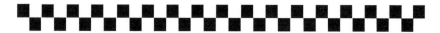

BANANA CREAM PIE

1 large ripe banana, sliced
2 (4-serving) packages vanilla pudding mix
2 cups cold milk
1 (8-ounce) tub whipped topping, thawed
1 (9-inch) pie crust, baked

In bottom of pie crust, place bananas. In large bowl, combine pudding mix and milk. Mix until thickened. Fold in whipped topping. Pour over bananas. Cover and chill 4 hours. Top with additional bananas if desired.

WHOLE LOT OF CHOCOLATE PIE

2 (4-serving) boxes chocolate fudge flavor pudding and pie filling
3½ cups milk
2 tablespoons butter or margarine
2 squares semi-sweet chocolate
1 (9-inch) pie shell, baked

In large saucepan, combine pie filling and milk. Add butter and chocolate. Cook over medium heat, stirring until a bubbling boil. Remove from heat. Cool 5 minutes. Mix well. Pour mixture into pie shell. Chill until set. Garnish with whipped topping.

SIMPLY PECAN PIE

3 eggs, slightly beaten

1 cup dark corn syrup

1 cup sugar

2 tablespoons butter or margarine, melted

1 teaspoon vanilla

1½ cups pecans

1 (9-inch) pie shell, unbaked

Preheat oven to 350 degrees. In large bowl, combine eggs, corn syrup, sugar, butter, and vanilla. Mix well. Stir in nuts. Pour mixture into pie shell. Bake 50 to 55 minutes. Makes 6 to 8 servings.

OLDIE RHUBARB PIE

1¼ cups sugar

⅓ cup all-purpose flour

4 cups rhubarb, cut into 1 inch pieces

2 tablespoons butter

2 (9-inch) pie shells

Preheat oven to 375 degrees. In large bowl, combine sugar and flour. Mix well. Add rhubarb, mix to coat. Let stand 20 minutes. Pour mixture into pie shell. Dot with butter. Top with crust, flute edges. Cover edges of crust with tin foil. Bake 25 minutes. Remove foil. Bake 25 minutes or until golden brown. Makes 6 to 8 servings.

Spray cupcake liners with non-stick cooking spray and the cupcakes can be removed without sticking to the paper.

LIKE GRANDMA'S CHERRY PIE

4 cups fresh or frozen tart red cherries

1 cup sugar

3 tablespoons quick cooking tapioca

1 teaspoon finely shredded lemon peel

1 tablespoon butter or margarine

1 (9-inch) pie shell

Preheat oven to 375 degrees. In large bowl, combine cherries, sugar, tapioca, and lemon peel. Mix well. Pour mixture into pie shell. Dot with butter. Top with crust, flute edges. Cover edge of crust with foil. Bake 30 minutes. Remove foil. Bake 25 minutes or until golden brown. Cool. Makes 6 to 8 servings.

ALMOST APPLE PIE

¾ cup sugar

½ cup flour

1 teaspoon baking powder

¼ teaspoon salt

1 egg, lightly beaten

1 teaspoon vanilla

2 cups sliced tart apples

1 (9-inch) pie shell

Preheat oven to 350 degrees. In medium bowl, combine sugar, flour, and baking powder and salt. Add egg and vanilla. Mix well. Fold in apples. In buttered 9-inch pie pan, pour mixture. Bake 30 minutes. Serve with ice cream or whipped topping if desired. Makes 6 servings.

PEANUT BUTTER & JELLY PIE

1 (8-ounce) tub whipped topping thawed
½ cup strawberry jelly
1 (3.4-ounce) package instant vanilla pudding mix
1 cup cold milk
½ cup peanut butter
1 (9-inch) prepared graham cracker crust

In small bowl, combine 1 cup whipped topping and jelly. Spread in bottom of pie crust. In medium bowl, combine pudding mix and milk. Stir until thickened. Add peanut butter. Mix until smooth. Fold in remaining whipped topping. Pour into crust. Cover and freeze 4 hours. Remove 10 minutes before serving.

PEACH PIE

2 (16-ounce) cans sliced peaches in light syrup
¼ cup lemon juice
1 cup sugar
1 (9-inch) prepared vanilla wafer pie crust

Drain peaches, reserve liquid and 14 peach slices. In blender, combine peaches and lemon juice until smooth, set aside. Add water to reserved peach juice to make 1½ cups. In medium saucepan over medium high heat, bring peach juice and sugar to a boil. Boil 2 minutes, stirring occasionally. Cool. In blender, add peach syrup to peach liquid. Blend well. Pour into pie crust. Arrange reserved peaches on top. Freeze 4 hours.

TROPICAL PIE

1 (4-serving) package instant vanilla pudding mix
1 cup cold milk
1 (8-ounce) can crushed pineapple, drained
½ cup flaked coconut
1 (9-inch) piecrust, baked

In medium bowl, combine pudding and milk. Mix until thickened. Add pineapple and coconut. Mix well. Pour into piecrust. Chill for 2 hours. Garnish with whipped topping if desired.

RED PEAR PIE

1¼ cups water
½ cup red cinnamon candies
⅓ cup sugar
3 tablespoons cornstarch
2 tablespoons lemon juice
3 (16-ounce) cans pear halves, drained, halved
1 (9-inch) pie crust, baked

In small saucepan over medium high heat, combine water and candies. Cook until candy dissolves. In small bowl, combine sugar and cornstarch. Slowly pour into candy mixture, cook until bubbly and thick, stirring constantly. Remove from heat, add lemon juice. Spread ¼ cup mixture in bottom of pie crust. Arrange half or pears in shell. Pour half of remaining candy mixture over pears. Repeat process. Cover and chill 4 hours.

BAKED PIE CRUST

1 cup flour
3 tablespoons sugar
½ cup butter or margarine

Preheat oven to 350 degrees. In medium bowl, combine all ingredients. Mix well. Press dough in 8- or 9-inch pie pan. Bake 10 to 15 minutes or until golden brown.

CHOCOLATE CRUMB CRUST

1¼ cups finely crushed chocolate cookies
½ cup sugar
¼ cup margarine, melted

In medium bowl, combine all ingredients. Mix well. Press mixture evenly on bottom and sides of 9-inch pie pan. Fill as desired.

GRAHAM CRACKER CRUST

1½ cups graham cracker crumbs
2 tablespoons sugar
6 tablespoons margarine, melted
⅛ teaspoon cinnamon

Preheat oven to 350 degrees. In medium bowl, combine all ingredients. Mix well. Press evenly in 9-inch pie pan. Bake for 10 minutes. Cool.

To divide a pie into five equal slices, first cut a "Y" into the pie. Then cut the two large pieces in half.

PRETZEL CRUST

1¼ cups crushed pretzels
½ cup butter or margarine, melted
¼ cup sugar

In medium bowl, combine all ingredients. Mix well. Press mixture firmly against bottom and sides of 9-inch pie pan. Chill until firm.

NUT PIE CRUST

1 cup chopped pecans
1½ sticks butter, softened
1½ cups flour
2 tablespoons sugar

Preheat oven to 350 degrees. In medium bowl, combine pecans, butter, flour, and sugar. Roll out and pat in 9-inch pie pan. Bake 15 to 20 minutes or until golden brown.

MERINGUE FOR PIE

4 egg whites
½ teaspoon cream of tartar
8 tablespoons sugar

In medium bowl, combine egg whites and cream of tartar. Beat until frothy with electric mixer. Add sugar 1 tablespoon at a time, beating until egg whites stand in stiff peaks. Top on pie. Bake as desired for pie.

ROOT BEER FLOAT CAKE

1 box white cake mix
1¼ cups root beer
2 eggs
¼ cup oil
Root Beer Frosting

Preheat oven to 350 degrees. In large bowl, combine all ingredients except frosting. Beat on low speed with electric mixer, than on high 2 minutes. Pour batter into greased 13 x 9 x 2-inch baking pan. Bake 35 or 40 minutes. Cool and frost.

ROOT BEER FROSTING

1 (1.3-ounce) packet whipped topping
½ cup chilled root beer

In small bowl, combine whipped topping and root beer. Beat until stiff peaks form. Frost cake. Chill.

IT'S A SECRET CHOCOLATE CAKE

1 box chocolate cake mix
½ cup unsweetened cocoa
3 eggs
1½ cup water
1 cup Miracle Whip®

Preheat oven to 350 degrees. In large bowl, combine cake mix and cocoa. Mix well. Add eggs, water, and Miracle Whip. Beat at medium speed with electric mixer until blended. Pour mixture into greased and floured 13 x 9 x 2-inch baking pan. Bake 30 to 40 minutes. Makes 12 servings.

CANDY CAKE

1 (14-ounce) can sweetened condensed milk
1 egg, slightly beaten
1 box yellow cake mix
1 (12-ounce) bag chocolate chips
6 chocolate covered toffee bars, broken into small pieces

Preheat oven to 350 degrees. In large bowl, combine milk and egg. Add cake mix, stir until blended. Pour into greased and floured 13 x 9 x 2-inch cake pan. Sprinkle candy pieces evenly on top. Bake for 30 to 35 minutes.

NUTS ABOUT APPLE CAKE
(Slow Cooker)

1 (21-ounce) can apple pie filling
1 box yellow cake mix
½ cup butter or margarine, melted
½ cup walnuts

In slow cooker, add apple pie filling. In large bowl, combine cake mix and butter. Mix until crumbly. Pour mixture over pie filling. Sprinkle nuts on top. Cover and cook on low 2½ to 3 hours. Makes 8 to 10 serving.

NICE 'N EASY CHOCOLATE CAKE

1 box German chocolate cake mix
3 eggs
1¼ cups water
⅓ cup oil
½ cup diced walnuts
½ cup semi-sweet chocolate pieces

Preheat oven to 350 degrees. In large bowl, combine cake mix, eggs, water, and oil. Beat on low speed with electric mixer until blended. Beat 2 minutes at high speed. Pour mixture into cooking sprayed 13 x 9-inch pan. Sprinkle nut and chocolate pieces over batter. Bake 30 to 40 minutes.

EVERYONE'S DUMP CAKE

1 (15¼ ounce) can cherry pie filling
1 (15¼ ounce) can crushed pineapple, with juice
1 box yellow cake mix
1 stick margarine, melted

Preheat oven to 350 degrees. Pour cherry pie filling in 8 x 11 x 2-inch baking dish. Top with crushed pineapple. Sprinkle cake mix over top. Pour butter over dry cake mix. Bake 35 to 40 minutes.

Test baking powder or baking soda by placing a teaspoon in hot water. If it fizzles, it is still good.

MOUTHWATERING POUND CAKE

1 pound butter
1 (16-ounce) package confectioners sugar
6 eggs
1½ teaspoons vanilla
3 cups sifted cake flour

Preheat oven to 350 degrees. In large bowl, combine butter and sugar. Beat until fluffy. Add eggs, one at a time, beating well after each egg. Add vanilla. Blend. Add flour gradually. Pour mixture into buttered floured 10-inch tube ban. Bake 1½ hours. Let cool in pan before removing cake. Serve with fresh fruit and whipped topping.

FLUFFY ANGEL CAKE

2 cups whipping cream
½ cup sugar
1½ tablespoons instant coffee
1 teaspoon vanilla
1 prepared angel food cake

In small bowl, combine whipping cream, sugar, coffee, and vanilla. Beat with electric mixer on high speed until mixture holds peaks. Frost top and sides of cake.

PUMPKIN CUPCAKES

1 box spice cake mix
1 (15-ounce) can pumpkin
3 large eggs
⅓ cup oil
⅓ cup water
cream cheese frosting

Preheat oven to 350 degrees. In large bowl, combine cake mix, pumpkin, eggs, oil, and water. Beat with electric mixer on medium speed for 2 minutes. Pour batter into 24 paper lined muffin cups three-fourths full. Bake 15 to 20 minutes. Cool. Frost cupcakes with cream cheese frosting. Makes 24 cupcakes.

DANDY DO LITTLE CAKES

1 box yellow cake mix
1 cup semi-sweet chocolate chips
2 tablespoons butter
3 tablespoons half and half
2 tablespoons light corn syrup

Preheat oven to 375 degrees. Prepare cake as directed on box. Spray 9 paper hot drink cups with cooking spray. Spoon batter in cups half full. Place on baking sheet. Bake 20 to 25 minutes. Cool. Turn out of cups onto serving plate. In small saucepan, combine chocolate and butter. Cook over low heat until chips melt. Add half and half and syrup. Cool slightly. Drizzle over cake.

PINEAPPLE CAKE

2 cups flour
1½ cups sugar
1 teaspoon baking soda
1 (8-ounce) can crushed pineapple
2 eggs
Sweet Glaze

Preheat oven to 350 degrees. In large bowl, combine flour, sugar, and baking soda. Add pineapple and eggs, mix until smooth. Pour into greased and floured 13 x 9 x 2-inch cake pan. Bake for 30 minutes. Top with Sweet Glaze while cake is still warm.

SWEET GLAZE

1 cup evaporated milk
½ cup butter
¾ cup sugar

In small saucepan over high heat, combine all ingredients. Boil 3 minutes. Pour immediately over cake.

ICE CREAM CAKE

12 ice cream sandwiches
2 cups whipped topping, thawed, divided
⅔ cup toffee bits, divided

Line 13 x 9 x 2-inch baking pan with wax paper. In pan, arrange 6 ice cream sandwiches in two rows. Spread 1 cup whipped topping over sandwiches. Sprinkle with ⅓ cup toffee bits. Arrange remaining ice cream sandwiches over toffee bits. Freeze 2 hours. Place cake on serving platter. Top with remaining topping and toffee bits.

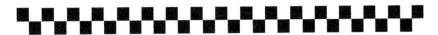

CHOCOLATE GLAZE

2 tablespoons butter or margarine
2 tablespoons coca
2 tablespoons water
1 cup confectioners sugar
¼ teaspoon almond extract

In small saucepan, melt butter over low heat. Add cocoa and water. Cook over low heat stirring constantly until smooth. Do not boil. Remove from heat. Add sugar gradually and almond extract. Beat until smooth. Spoon glaze over cake, allowing to drizzle down sides of cake.

WHITE FROSTING GLAZE

2 cups confectioners sugar
3 tablespoons milk
¼ teaspoon vanilla

In medium bowl, combine all ingredients. Beat until smooth. Drizzle over cooled cake.

CREAM CHEESE FROSTING

1 (3-ounce) package cream cheese
¼ cup butter or margarine
1 teaspoon vanilla
2 cups sifted confectioners sugar

In medium bowl, beat cream cheese, butter, and vanilla, until light and fluffy. Gradually add sugar, beating till smooth. Frost cake.

VANILLA FROSTING FOR CAKE

1 cup sifted confectioners sugar
2 tablespoons butter, softened
½ teaspoon vanilla
1 tablespoon milk

In small bowl, combine sugar, butter, and vanilla. Beat with electric mixer on medium speed. Add milk ¼ teaspoon at a time until desired consistency. Frost cake.

QUICK CHOCOLATE FROSTING

6 tablespoons butter
6 tablespoons milk
1½ cups sugar
1 cup milk chocolate chips

In medium saucepan, combine butter, milk, and sugar, over low heat. Cook and stir, bringing mixture to a boil. Cook 2 minutes. Place chocolate chips in medium bowl. Pour hot mixture over chips. Beat until smooth.

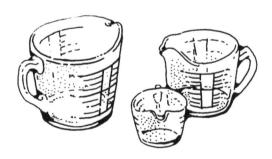

CHOCOLATE COOKIES

¾ cup butter, softened

½ cup sugar

1 egg yolk

1 teaspoon almond extract

1½ cups flour

¼ cup unsweetened cocoa

Preheat oven to 375 degrees. In large bowl, combine butter, sugar, egg yolk, and almond extract. Beat with electric mixer for 3 minutes. Gradually add flour and cocoa. Mix well. Shape in1 inch balls. Place 1-inch apart on lightly greased cookie sheet. Flatten slightly. Bake 8 to 9 minutes. Can be decorated with confectioners sugar or frosting. Makes 3 dozen.

CHOCOLATE DROP COOKIES

1 box chocolate cake mix

1 cup semi-sweet chocolate chips

2 eggs

½ cup Miracle Whip®

½ cup chopped walnuts

Preheat oven to 350 degrees. In large bowl, combine all ingredients. Mix with electric mixer on medium speed until blended. Drop by rounded teaspoonful onto greased cookie sheet. Bake 10 to 12 minutes. Makes 4 dozen.

NOTE: Batter will be very thick.

MAGICAL COOKIE BARS

½ cup butter or margarine

1½ cups graham cracker crumbs

1 (14-ounce) can sweetened condensed milk

2 cups semi-sweet chocolate chips

1⅓ cups flaked coconut

1 cup chopped nuts

Preheat oven to 350 degrees. In 13 x 9-inch baking pan, melt butter in oven. Sprinkle graham crumbs over butter. Pour milk evenly over crumbs. Top with chocolate, coconut, and nuts. Press down firmly with fork. Bake 25 to 30 minutes. Cool, cut into bars.

NO BAKE ALMOND COOKIES

1 (16-ounce) package almond bark

½ cup crunchy peanut butter

1 cup salted peanuts

1 cup miniature marshmallows

1½ cups Rice Krispies®

In large bowl, add bark. Microwave on high 2 minutes. Stir. Add peanut butter, peanuts, and marshmallows. Stir in Rice Krispies. Drop by teaspoon on wax paper. Cool.

COCONUT COOKIES

2 egg whites
½ teaspoon vanilla
⅔ cup sugar
1⅓ cups flaked coconut

Preheat oven to 325 degrees. In medium bowl, beat egg whites and vanilla until soft peaks form. Gradually add sugar, beating until stiff peaks form. Fold in coconut. Drop from teaspoon 1½ inches apart onto cooking sprayed cookie sheet. Bake 20 minutes. Cool. Makes 20 to 24 cookies.

YOU LIKE'M COOKIES

1 (14-ounce) can sweetened condensed milk
¾ cup peanut butter
2 cups biscuit baking mix
1 teaspoon vanilla
sugar

Preheat oven to 375 degrees. In large bowl, combine milk and peanut butter. Beat until smooth. Add biscuit mix and vanilla. Mix well. Shape mixture into 1-inch balls. Roll in sugar. Place 2 inches apart on ungreased baking sheet. Flatten with fork. Bake 6 to 8 minutes or until lightly browned. Makes 3 to 5 dozen.

KIDS CAN MAKE IT COOKIE

1 (16-ounce) package chocolate bark
24 Ritz® crackers
1 cup peanut butter

In small saucepan, melt bark, keep on low heat so it doesn't harden. Spread peanut butter on puffy side of cracker. Add another cracker to make sandwich. Dip cracker sandwich into melted bark, set on wax paper until dry and hardened. Makes 12 cookies.

IS IT CHEESECAKE OR A COOKIE?

2 (18-ounce) rolls chocolate chip cookie dough
2 (8-ounce) packages cream cheese, softened
1 cup sugar
1 egg
1 tablespoon vanilla

Preheat oven to 350 degrees. In ungreased 13 x 9 x 2-inch baking pan, spread 1 roll of cookie dough in bottom. In medium bowl, combine cream cheese, sugar, egg, and vanilla. Mix until smooth. Pour over cookie dough. Slice remaining cookie dough into small pieces. Sprinkle over cream cheese mixture. Bake 35 minutes. Cool before refrigerating.

LOOKS LIKE ICE CREAM CONE COOKIES

1⅓ cups confectioners sugar
2 tablespoons butter, no substitutes, softened
¼ teaspoon vanilla
¼ teaspoon salt
2 tablespoons sweetened condensed milk
1 (6-ounce) package Bugles®

In small bowl, cream sugar and butter. Add vanilla and salt. Mix well. Add condensed milk. Mix well. Shape mixture into ½-inch balls. Place one ball in the end of Bugles. Decorate if desired with colored sprinkles, melted chocolate, or small candies. Makes 2½ dozen.

If cookies get too hard put them in a plastic bag with a piece of bread and leave overnight. The next morning, the cookies should be soft.

MALTED COOKIES

⅔ cup butter or margarine

½ cup confectioners sugar

2¼ cups flour

⅔ cup crushed malted milk ball candies

½ cup malted milk mix

1 teaspoon vanilla

1 (11.5-ounce) package milk chocolate chips

In medium bowl, cream butter and sugar. In medium bowl, combine flour, candies, and malted milk mix. Add to creamed mixture. Mix well. Knead dough, shape into ball. Wrap in plastic wrap and chill overnight. Preheat oven to 350 degrees. Shape dough into 1-inch balls and place on ungreased baking pan. Bake 15 minutes or until golden brown. In small saucepan over low heat, melt chocolate chips. Remove from heat. Coat cookies in chocolate. Place on wax paper to cool. Makes 4 dozen.

LEMON COOKIES

1 (18.25-ounce) box lemon flavored cake mix

1 (4 ounce) tub whipped topping, thawed

1 egg

½ cup confectioners sugar

Preheat oven to 350 degrees. In large bowl, combine cake mix, whipped topping, and egg. Roll 1-inch ball of dough in sugar. On greased cookie sheet, place balls 2 inches apart. Bake 10 to12 minutes, or until golden brown. Makes 6 dozen.

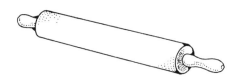

OATMEAL COOKIES WITH A TWIST

1 (16-ounce) package pound cake mix

2 eggs

¾ cup vegetable oil

1 teaspoon vanilla

½ teaspoon ground cinnamon

1 cup quick cooking oats

¾ cup chocolate covered raisins

Preheat oven to 375 degrees. In large bowl, combine cake mix, eggs, oil, vanilla, and cinnamon. Beat until smooth. Fold in oats and raisins. On ungreased cookie sheet, drop dough by teaspoon 2-inches apart. Bake 8 to 10 minutes or until edges or golden brown. Makes 4 dozen.

MACAROONS

2⅔ cups flaked coconut

⅔ cup sugar

6 tablespoons flour

¼ teaspoon salt

4 egg whites

1 teaspoon almond extract

Preheat oven to 325 degrees. In large bowl, combine coconut, sugar, flour, and salt. Add egg whites and almond extract. Mix well. Drop by tablespoon onto greased and floured cookie sheet. Bake 20 minutes or until edges are golden brown. Makes 2 dozen.

BUTTERSCOTCH NO BAKE COOKIES

1 (12-ounce) package butterscotch morsels
1 cup crunchy peanut butter
4 cups plain corn flakes

In a large saucepan over low heat, combine morsels and peanut butter. Stir until melted. Remove from heat. Fold in corn flakes. Mix well. Drop by tablespoon onto wax paper. Cool and serve.

NO BAKE HONEY COOKIES

½ cup honey
½ cup sugar
1 cup peanut butter
2 cups crispy rice cereal

In large saucepan over medium heat, combine honey and sugar. Bring to a boil, remove from heat. Add peanut butter. Mix well. Add cereal, stir to coat. Drop by tablespoons onto wax paper covered baking sheet. Freeze till set. Makes 20 to 24 cookies.

FROSTING FOR COOKIES

¼ cup margarine
1½ teaspoons vanilla
3 cups confectioners sugar
¼ cup milk

In small bowl, combine all ingredients with electric mixer on low speed. Beat until smooth. Tint with food coloring if desired.

APPLE SOPAPILLAS

6 (8-inch) flour tortillas
12 tablespoons apple pie filling
3 tablespoons confectioners sugar
oil

On each flour tortilla, place 2 tablespoons apple pie filling. Fold as you would a burrito. Deep fry in 1 inch of oil, seam down until golden brown on both sides. Drain on paper towel. Dust with confectioners sugar. Makes 6 servings.

RAISIN PEANUT SQUARES

⅓ cup butter or margarine
4 cups miniature marshmallows
5 cups crisp rice cereal
1½ cups raisins
1 cup peanuts

In large bowl, combine butter and marshmallows. Cover and micro-wave at high 2 to 3 minutes. Add cereal, raisins, and peanuts. Mix well to coat. Press mixture into cooking sprayed 13 x 9-inch pan. Cool. Cut into squares. Makes 2 to 4 dozen squares.

CRUNCH SQUARES

¼ cup butter or margarine
3 cups miniature marshmallows
5 cups honey graham cereal
1 cup roasted peanuts

In 2½-quart casserole, microwave butter at high for 30 seconds. Add marsh mallows. Microwave at high 1 minute. Stir mixture to blend marshmallows. Add cereal and peanuts. Press mixture into 9-inch square pan. Chill. Cut into squares.

SWEET AND NUTTY BARS

½ cup butter or margarine

1½ cups graham cracker crumbs

1 (14-ounce) can sweetened condensed milk

1 (12-ounce) package semisweet chocolate chips

1⅓ cups flaked coconut

1 cup chopped pecans

Preheat oven to 350 degrees. In 13 x 9 x 2-inch baking pan, place butter, put in oven until melted. Sprinkle graham cracker crumbs over butter. Pour milk over crumbs. Layer chocolate chips, coconut, and pecans. Using a fork, press ingredients down. Bake 25 minutes.

CARROT AND CREAM CHEESE BARS

⅓ cup oil

3 eggs

1½ cups applesauce

1 box carrot 'n spice cake mix

1 cup raisins

1 (16 ounce) can ready to spread cream cheese frosting

Preheat oven to 350 degrees. In large bowl, combine oil, eggs, and applesauce. Beat at low speed with electric mixer. Add cake mix, blend until moistened. Beat 2 minutes. Stir in raisins. Pour mixture into greased and floured 9-inch pans. Bake 25 to 35 minutes. Cool. Frost with cream cheese. Cut into bars. Makes 36.

COOKIE BARS

35 chocolate sandwich cookies
¼ cup butter or margarine, melted
1 (7½-ounce) jar marshmallow cream
½ cup semisweet chocolate chips

Preheat oven to 350 degrees. Finely crush 27 cookies. In small bowl, combine crushed cookies and butter. Press into greased 8 x 8-inch baking pan. Spread marshmallow cream over cookie mixture. Coarsely crush remaining cookies. Sprinkle cookies and chips over marshmallow. Bake 16 to18 minutes. Cool before cutting. Makes 16 servings.

BROWNIES

¾ cup butter or margarine
4 squares unsweetened baking chocolate
2 cups sugar
3 eggs
1 teaspoon vanilla
1 cup flour

Preheat oven to 350 degrees. In large saucepan over medium heat, melt butter and chocolate. Remove from heat. Add sugar, eggs, and vanilla. Mix well. Add flour. Stir until well blended. In greased 1½-quart baking pan, pour batter. Bake 30 to 35 minutes. Makes 24 servings.

Immediately cover your brownies when they come out of the oven. This keeps them moist.

NO TROUBLE CHOCOLATE TRUFFLES

4 ounces semi sweet chocolate

3½ ounces almond paste

1 tablespoon hazelnut syrup

1 tablespoon strong hot coffee

2 tablespoons confectioner's sugar

In a blender container, combine chocolate and almond paste. Cover. Blend until smooth. Add syrup and coffee. Mix well. Form dough into ¾-inch balls. Place balls on an ungreased cookie sheet. Top with confectioners sugar. Chill 1 to 2 hours. Makes 8 to 10 balls.

CEREAL BARS

1 cup white corn syrup

1 cup sugar

¾ cup chunky peanut butter

6 cups corn flakes cereal

1 (12-ounce) package semisweet chocolate chips

1 (12-ounce) package butterscotch chips

In large saucepan over medium high heat, combine syrup and sugar. Stir constantly until it boils. Reduce heat. Add peanut butter, mix until smooth. Remove form heat. Add cereal, stir to coat. In buttered 13 x 9 x 2-inch pan, pour mixture. In medium saucepan over low heat, melt chips. Pour over cereal mixture. Cool. Cut into squares.

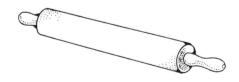

MARSHMALLOW BARS

10 whole graham crackers
1 package fudge brownie mix
2 cups miniature marshmallows
1 cup semisweet chocolate chips

Preheat oven to 350 degrees. In 13 x 9 x 2-inch baking pan, line with graham crackers. Prepare brownies according to package directions. Pour batter over crackers. Bake 30 minutes. Sprinkle marshmallows and chips over brownies. Bake 5 minutes or until marshmallows are toasted.

CRAZY BARS

1 cup light corn syrup
1 cup sugar
½ cup peanut butter
5 cups crispy rice cereal
2 cups pretzel sticks
1 cup plain M&M's®

In large saucepan over medium high heat, combine corn syrup and sugar. Cook until sugar dissolves. Remove from heat, add peanut butter. Mix well. Add cereal, pretzels, and M&M's. Stir until coated. Press mixture into greased 13 x 9 x 2-inch pan. Cut into squares.

 Brown quick-cooking oats in a little butter, then use them as a substitute for chopped nuts in cookie recipes.

TAKE A HIKE BARS

¾ cup packed brown sugar
½ cup butter or margarine, softened
1 teaspoon baking powder
1 teaspoon vanilla
2 eggs
1 cup flour
1 cup trail mix with chocolate candy pieces

Preheat oven to 325 degrees. In large bowl, cream brown sugar, butter, baking powder, and vanilla. Add eggs. Mix well. Add flour, stir until blended. Fold in trail mix. In greased 8 x 8-inch pan, spread mixture. Bake 30 to 35 minutes. Makes 24 bars.

TURTLE BARS

1½ cups firmly packed brown sugar, divided
½ cup butter or margarine, softened
2 cups flour
1 cup chopped pecans
⅔ cup butter or margarine, softened
1 cup milk chocolate chips

Preheat oven to 350 degrees. In large bowl, combine 1 cup brown sugar and ½ cup butter. Mix until creamy. Gradually add flour. Beat until well blended. In ungreased 13 x 9 x 2-inch baking pan, press mixture. Sprinkle with pecans. In small saucepan over medium high heat, combine ⅔ cup butter and ½ cup brown sugar. Bring to a boil, stirring constantly. Boil 30 seconds. Remove from heat and pour over mixture in pan. Bake 18 minutes. Sprinkle chips immediately over top. Let stand 3 minutes. Swirl chocolate with knife. Cover and chill until chocolate hardens.

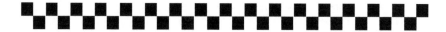

NO BAKE CHEESECAKE

1 (8-ounce) package cream cheese, softened
⅓ cup sugar
1 (8-ounce) tub whipped topping
1 prepared graham cracker pie crust

In large bowl, combine cream cheese and sugar. Mix well. Fold in whipped topping. Pour into pie crust. Cover and chill 3 hours.

MAKE A FRESH TART

1 (4-serving) box strawberry gelatin
1 cup boiling water
½ cup cold water
1 (21-ounce) can strawberry fruit pie filling
1 teaspoon lemon juice
8 tart shells, baked

In large bowl, dissolve gelatin in boiling water. Stir in cold water, strawberry fruit filling and lemon juice. Chill until slightly thickened, then spoon into tart shells. Chill until firm. Shells can be purchased in stores.

CHOCOLATE MOUSSE TARTS

1 (14-ounce) can sweetened condensed milk
1 cup cold water
1 (4-serving) package instant chocolate pudding mix
2 cups whipped topping, thawed
2 (4-ounce) packages single serve graham cracker
    pie crusts

In large bowl, combine condensed milk, water, and pudding. Mix well. Chill 15 minutes. Fold in whipped topping. Pour into pie crusts. Chill until serving. Makes 12 tarts.

PEACH CRISP

2 (15¼-ounce) cans sliced peaches, drained

2 (1.6-ounce) packages cinnamon and spice instant oatmeal

⅓ cup flour

⅓ cup butter or margarine, melted

Preheat oven to 425 degrees. In buttered 2-quart baking dish, pour peaches. In medium bowl, combine oatmeal and flour. Stir in butter. Mix well. Sprinkle over peaches. Bake 15 minutes. Makes 6 servings.

APPLE CRISP

⅔ cup firmly packed brown sugar

½ cup flour

1 cup quick cooking oatmeal

½ cup butter or margarine, melted

1 (15-ounce) can apple pie filling

Preheat oven to 350 degrees. In medium bowl, combine brown sugar, flour, and oatmeal. Stir in butter. Mix well. In buttered 8 x 8-inch baking pan, press three-fourths of oatmeal mixture. Pour pie filling over mixture. Top with remaining oatmeal mixture. Bake 30 to 35 minutes or until lightly brown.

GOOD OLD CHERRY COBBLER
(Slow Cooker)

1 (16-ounce) can cherry pie filling
1¾ cups cake mix, from two layer box
1 egg
3 tablespoons evaporated milk
½ teaspoon cinnamon

In slow cooker, add cherry pie filling. Cover. Cook on high 30 minutes. In medium bowl, combine cake mix, egg, milk, and cinnamon. Mix until crumbly. Spoon mixture over hot cherry filling. Cover. Cook on low 2 to 3 hours. Makes 8 servings.

ALMOST ECLAIRS

1 box deluxe yellow cake mix
2 (5-ounce) cans vanilla pudding
chocolate fudge topping

Preheat oven to 350 degrees. Prepare cake as directed on package. Pour into 13 x 9-inch pan, bake as directed. Cool. Cut cake into 4½ x 1½-inch pieces. Cut each piece in half lengthwise. Spread one tablespoon of pudding between split cake top with chocolate fudge. Keep in refrigerator.

CUT-IT-SHORT TORTE

1 box pudding devils food cake mix
1(8-ounce) tub whipped topping, thawed
1 (21 ounce) can cherry pie filling

Preheat oven to 350 degrees. Prepare cake mix as directed on package. Pour mixture into greased and floured 10-inch tube pan. Bake as directed. Cool. Split cake into 3 layers. Spread ⅓ of whipped topping, then ⅓ of pie filling between each layer and top. Chill until set.

ICE CREAM FUDGE DESSERT
(Homemade Blessings)

19 ice cream sandwiches
1 (12-ounce) tub whipped topping, thawed
1(11¾-ounce) jar hot fudge ice cream topping
1 cup salted peanuts

In 13 x 9-inch baking pan, place one whole and one half sandwich along short side. Arrange eight sandwiches in opposite direction in pan. Spread with half of whipped topping. Spoon fudge topping by teaspoonfuls onto whipped topping. Sprinkle half of the peanuts over top. Repeat layers with remaining ice cream sandwiches, whipped topping, and peanuts. Pan will be full. Cover and freeze. Remove from freezer 20 minutes before serving. Makes 10 to 12 servings.

CHOC-A-BLOC

1 box deep chocolate cake mix
1 quart brick mint chip ice cream
chocolate topping

Preheat oven to 350 degrees. Prepare cake as directed on package. Spread batter in oiled and floured 15½ x 10½ x 1-inch jelly pan. Bake 20 to 25 minutes. Cut cake into serving size squares. Put a slice of ice cream between 2 pieces of cake. Cover with chocolate topping. Serve at once or freeze.

 Use a doily to make a snowflake pattern on top of an unfrosted cake. Place the doily on top of the cake and sift confectioner's sugar onto the doily until all the spaces in the doily are filled with sugar. Carefully remove the doily to reveal your design.

COOKIES & CREAM DESSERT

1 (4-serving) package instant vanilla pudding mix
2 cups cold milk
15 chocolate sandwich cookies, broken into chunks
1 (8-ounce) carton whipped topping, thawed

In large bowl, combine pudding and milk. Mix until thickened. Add cookies and whipped topping. Mix well. Chill until served. Makes 6 servings.

EMERGENCY BLUEBERRY DESSERT

1 (21-ounce) can blueberry fruit pie filling
2 cups frozen whipped topping, thawed
¼ cup coconut, toasted

In medium bowl, fold in pie filling and whipped topping. Spoon mixture into dessert dishes. Sprinkle coconut over top. Chill. Makes 6 servings.

BLUE ANGEL DESSERT

1 (8-ounce) package cream cheese, softened
1 cup confectioners sugar
1 (8-ounce) tub whipped topping, thawed
1 angel food cake, cut into 1-inch cubes
2 (21-ounce) cans blueberry pie filling

In large bowl, combine cream cheese and sugar, until smooth. Add whipped topping. Fold in cake cubes. Mix well. In an ungreased 13 x 9 x 2-inch pan, pour mixture. Top with pie filling. Cover and chill for 2 hours. Makes 14 servings.

CAPPUCCINO CUPS

8 teaspoons instant cappuccino powder
2 (3-ounce) packages cream cheese, softened
4 teaspoons sugar
2 cups whipped topping
4 slices pound cake, cubed
½ cup semisweet chocolate chips

In medium bowl, cream cappuccino powder, cream cheese, and sugar. Add whipped topping. Beat until smooth. In four dessert dishes, divide cake. Pour cappuccino mixture over cake. Top with chocolate chips. If desired top with whipped topping and additional chocolate chips. Makes 4 servings.

BERRY PARFAITS

1 cup blueberries
1 cup raspberries
2 (8-ounce) containers strawberry yogurt
whipped topping

In 4 parfait glasses, layer blueberries, yogurt, raspberries, and yogurt again. Top with whipped topping.

CHOCOLATE COVERED STRAWBERRIES

3 ounces semisweet chocolate
1½ teaspoons vegetable shortening
30 strawberries, washed and dried

In a small saucepan over low heat, melt chocolate and shortening. Dip strawberries in melted chocolate. Place on waxed paper. Chill till serving time. Makes 30 pieces.

ICE CREAM PIZZA

½ (20-ounce) package refrigerated sugar cookie dough
1 quart vanilla ice cream, softened
assorted fresh or canned fruit, sliced
½ cup caramel ice cream topping

Preheat oven to 350 degrees. On ungreased 12-inch pizza pan, press dough, covering entire surface. Bake 12 to 14 minutes. Cool. Spread ice cream over cookie. Arrange fruit over ice cream. Drizzle with caramel topping over top. Freeze 1 hour.

ICE CREAM SANDWICHES

12 large chocolate chip cookies
1 pint vanilla ice cream, softened
miniature chocolate chips

Top 6 cookies with scoop of ice cream. Top with remaining cookies, press gently. Roll edges of ice cream in chocolate chips. Freeze 1 hour.

HOMEMADE ICE CREAM
(Get Me Out of the Kitchen)

6 eggs
1 cup sugar
4 tablespoons white corn syrup
1 (14-ounce) can sweetened condensed milk
Milk to fill a one gallon ice cream freezer container
    4 inches from top

In large bowl, using electric mixer, beat eggs and sugar until blended. Add syrup and milks. Pour into freezer container and fix according to freezer instructions.

BERRY AND BANANA POPSICLES

2 large bananas, peeled and sliced
1 (10-ounce) package sweetened strawberries, thawed
⅔ cup water

In blender, combine all ingredients. Cover, blend until smooth and creamy. Pour mixture into popsicle molds and freeze. Makes 8 popsicles.

PINA COLADA ICE CREAM

1 (14-ounce) can sweetened condensed milk
1 cup milk
½ cup frozen pineapple juice
2 tablespoons lime juice
¾ cup toasted flaked coconut

In medium bowl, combine milks, pineapple juice, and lime juice. Mix well. Pour mixture into 9 x 9-inch baking dish. Cover, freeze until almost firm. Break mixture into large chilled bowl. Beat with electric mixer until smooth but not melted. Return to baking dish. Cover and freeze until firm. Makes 6 to 8 servings.

FAMILY FAVORITE SUNDAE

2 (1-ounce) squares semi-sweet chocolate, chopped
2 tablespoons creamy peanut butter
1 (14-ounce) can condensed milk
2 tablespoons milk
1 teaspoon vanilla
1 quart vanilla ice cream

In medium saucepan, combine chocolate, peanut butter, condensed milk, and milk. Cook over medium low heat, stirring constantly until chocolate melts. Add vanilla. Remove from heat. Cool slightly. Serve over ice cream. Makes 6 servings.

PEACHY KEEN SHERBET

½ cup water

2 tablespoons orange flavored instant breakfast drink
  powder

¼ teaspoon almond extract

2 (10-ounce) packages frozen peach slices

In blender container, combine water, drink powder, and almond
extract. Break apart peaches. Add to blender. Cover and blend on high
speed till smooth. Spoon into individual sherbet dishes. Freeze until
solid. Makes 4 servings.

STRAWBERRY SHERBET

1(10-ounce) package frozen sweetened strawberries,
  thawed

1 (5-ounce) can evaporated milk

1 cup ice cubes

¼ cup sugar

1 teaspoon lemon juice

In blender, combine all ingredients. Cover and blend until smooth.
Pour into 2 ice cream dishes. Freeze until firm. Makes 2 servings.

RICE PUDDING

1 cup cooked long grain rice

1 cup milk

5 teaspoons sugar

½ teaspoon vanilla

In medium saucepan over medium heat, combine rice, milk, and sugar.
Cook uncovered for 20 minutes or until thickened, stirring often.
Remove form heat, stir in vanilla. Pour into serving dishes. Serve hot
or cold. Makes 2 servings.

FABULOUS CREAMY RICE PUDDING
(Slow Cooker)

3 cups cooked white rice

½ cup raisins

1 (14-ounce) can condensed milk

1 (12-ounce) can evaporated milk

1 tablespoon sugar

1 teaspoon cinnamon

Spray inside slow cooker with cooking spray. Combine rice, raisins, and milks. Mix well. Cover and cook on low 3 to 4 hours or until liquid is absorbed. Stir in sugar and cinnamon. Makes 8 servings.

CHOCOLATE FANS PUDDING

1 (4-serving) box chocolate pudding

¼ cup milk

½ cup semi-sweet chocolate pieces

1 teaspoon vanilla

1 cup whipping cream, whipped

Prepare pudding according to box, but adding ¼ cup milk. Add chocolate pieces, stirring till melted. Cool. Add vanilla. Beat mixture until fluffy. Fold in whipped cream. Spoon mixture in serving dishes. Chill. Makes 6 to 8 servings.

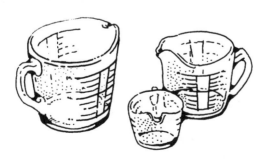

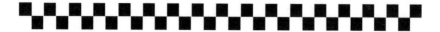

BUTTERSCOTCH PUDDING

1 cup packed dark brown sugar

¼ cup water

½ stick butter, sliced

1 cup half and half

1 cup milk

3 tablespoons cornstarch

1½ teaspoons vanilla

In large saucepan over medium high heat, combine sugar and water. Cook until sugar dissolves. Add butter. In small bowl, combine half and half, milk, and cornstarch, add to sugar. Boil 5 minutes, stirring constantly. Remove from heat, add vanilla. Pour into serving dishes. Cover and chill 1 hour. Makes 4 servings.

FAVORITE PRALINES

2 cups firmly packed light brown sugar

¾ cup half and half

3 tablespoons butter

1½ cups chopped pecans

⅛ teaspoon ground cinnamon

In large mixing bowl, combine sugar, half and half, and butter. Microwave at high 9 to 12 minutes or until a small amount dropped in cold water forms a soft ball. Add pecans and cinnamon. Mix well. Cool until lukewarm. Beat until smooth. Drop by teaspoonfuls onto waxed paper. Makes 20 to 24 pralines.

To use hard brown sugar, scrape the lump on a cheese grater to shave off the amount that is needed.

MOCHA PEANUT CLUSTERS

1 cup semi-sweet chocolate morsels

⅓ cup butter or margarine

16 large marshmallows

1 tablespoon instant coffee granules

2 cups salted peanuts

In 2 quart casserole, place chocolate. Microwave at medium 1½ minutes to melt. Add butter and marshmallows. Microwave at high 1½ minutes. Stir until creamy. Add instant coffee. Stir in peanuts. Drop by teaspoonfuls onto waxed paper. Chill. Makes 24 pieces.

GIA'S DELICIOUS PEANUT BRITTLE

3 cups raw peanuts

2 cups sugar

1 cup Karo® syrup

1 tablespoon butter or margarine

1 teaspoon vanilla

1 tablespoon baking soda

2 teaspoons salt

In large heavy saucepan, combine peanuts, sugar, Karo syrup, and butter. Cook over medium heat, stir continuously until liquid state and boiling. Then stir frequently for 10 minutes or until golden brown. Remove from heat. Add vanilla, soda, and salt. Beat for a few seconds. Pour mixture into buttered jelly roll pans. Shake pans to spread, so bubbles won't break down, it keeps it crunchy. Let harden.

PEANUT BUTTER FUDGE

1 (14-ounce) can sweetened condensed milk
1 (11-ounce) package butterscotch pieces
2½ cups miniature marshmallows
½ cup creamy peanut butter
1 teaspoon vanilla

In large saucepan over low heat, combine milk, butterscotch pieces, and marshmallows until melted. Mix well. Remove from heat. Stir in peanut butter and vanilla. Mix well. Pour into buttered 8 x 8-inch pan. Cover and chill.

FOOLPROOF EVERYTIME FUDGE

3 cups sweet chocolate chips
1 (14-ounce) can sweetened condensed milk
1 cup chopped nuts
1½ teaspoons vanilla

In medium saucepan, combine chocolate chips and milk. Cook over medium heat until mixture melts. Remove from heat. Add nuts and vanilla. Mix well. Spread evenly into 9-inch square pan sprayed with cooking spray. Chill until firm. Cut into squares.

FUSS FREE FUDGE

1 (14-ounce) can sweetened condensed milk
3 cups semisweet chocolate chips
1 cup peanut butter chips
1½ teaspoons vanilla

In large saucepan over medium heat, combine condensed milk and chocolate chips. Melt chips. Remove from heat. Add peanut butter chips and vanilla. Mix well. Pour into buttered 8 x 8-inch pan. Cover and chill 2 hours.

FUDGE SURPRISE

1 cup plus 3 tablespoons peanut butter

1 cup butter, no substitutions

3½ cups confectioners sugar

3 tablespoons cocoa powder

1 tablespoon vanilla

In large saucepan over medium heat, combine peanut butter and butter. Cook until blended. Remove from heat. Add sugar, cocoa, and vanilla. Mix well. Pour into buttered 8 x 8-inch pan. Freeze for 30 minutes.

S'MORES FUDGE

1⅓ cups semisweet chocolate chips

⅔ cup sweetened condensed milk

1⅓ cups miniature marshmallows, divided

1 teaspoon vanilla

2 graham crackers, broken into small pieces

In large saucepan over low heat, combine chocolate chips and milk. Stir constantly until melted. Remove from heat, cool 2 minutes. Add half of marshmallows and vanilla. Mix well. Pour into buttered 8 x 8-inch pan. Top with remaining marshmallows and graham cracker pieces. Cover and chill 3 hours.

PEANUT CLUSTERS
(Slow Cooker)

2 pounds white candy coating, chopped
1 (12-ounce) package semisweet chocolate chips
1 (4-ounce) bar milk chocolate
1 (24-ounce) jar dry roasted peanuts

In slow cooker, combine white candy coating, chocolate chips, and milk chocolate. Cover and cook on low 3 hours. Stir often. Add peanuts to melted chocolate. Mix well. Drop by tablespoon onto wax paper. Cool to set. Makes 3½ dozen.

SHOESTRING CANDIES

1 (11-ounce) package chocolate chips
3 tablespoons creamy peanut butter
2 cups shoestring potatoes

In large saucepan, melt chocolate chips and peanut butter over low heat. Stir constantly. Remove from heat. Add shoestring potatoes. Mix well. Drop by tablespoon onto wax paper. Cool.

CHOCOLATE SURPRISE PASTRIES

1 sheet frozen puff pastry dough, thawed
1 (6-ounce) package semisweet chocolate chips
¼ cup chopped walnuts
confectioners sugar

Preheat oven to 425 degrees. Roll pastry sheet to 12-inch square. Cut into four 6-inch squares. In center of each square, place ¼ cup chocolate chips and 1 tablespoon walnuts. Bring edges together, twist to close. Place on ungreased cookie sheet. Bake 10 to 12 minutes or until golden brown. Sprinkle with confectioners sugar. Makes 4 servings.

CANDY FOR DESSERT

2 (8-ounce) cans crushed pineapple, drained
1 (8-ounce) tub whipped topping, thawed
3 apples, peeled, cubed
3 (2-ounce) Snicker® candy bars, chopped

In medium bowl, combine pineapple and whipped topping. Fold in apples and candy. Cover and chill 2 hours before serving. Makes 8 servings.

IN A PINCH CANDY

14 ounces chocolate candy coating
2½ cups crispy rice cereal

In medium sauce pan over low heat, melt candy coating. Add cereal, stir to coat. Drop by teaspoon onto wax paper. Cool to harden. Makes 3½ dozen.

GREEN WITH ENVY CANDY

1 (5-ounce) can evaporated milk
1 (3-ounce) package pistachio pudding mix (not instant)
1 cup sugar
2 tablespoons butter or margarine
½ cup chopped pistachios

In medium saucepan over medium heat, combine milk, pudding, and sugar. Bring to a boil and boil 5 minutes, stirring constantly. Remove from heat, stir in butter. Pour mixture into medium bowl, mix with electric mixer 5 minutes. Fold in pistachios. Drop by teaspoon onto wax paper lined cookie sheet. Refrigerate until firm. Makes 4 dozen.

NOT TOO NUTS CANDY

1 (12-ounce) package semisweet chocolate chips
3 tablespoons ground cinnamon
1 cup oyster crackers
1 cup cashews

In medium saucepan over low heat, melt chocolate chips. Stir in cinnamon. Add crackers and cashews. Mix well. Drop by tablespoon onto wax paper. Cool. Makes 2½ dozen.

FUN CHOCOLATE FONDUE
(Slow Cooker)

1 (12-ounce) package semisweet chocolate chips
1 (14-ounce) can sweetened condensed milk
½ cup half and half
1 teaspoon vanilla
assorted fruit, cake, and marshmallows

In slow cooker, combine chips, milk, half and half, and vanilla. Cover and cook on high 3 hours. Stirring 2 times during cooking. Serve with fruit, angel food and pound cake, and marshmallows.

TECHNIQUES, TIPS & TABLE MANNERS

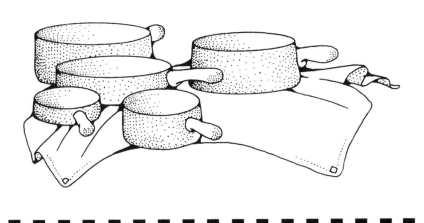

Adapt Most Recipes to a Slow Cooker for Hassle Free Cooking

CROCK POT® AND SLOW COOKERS ARE THE SAME

YOU CAN PREPARE just about any type of meal in a Slow Cooker. There is nothing easier then putting ingredients into a Slow Cooker in the morning, and coming home to a hot cooked meal. Here are some tips to help adapt your recipes for successful cooking in your Slow Cooker. Several factors can affect your recipes, so REMEMBER THESE TIPS.

Cooking time in all recipes are approximations, affected by how much food is in the cooker, humidity, the temperature of the ingredients when you add them; so note that cooking times in the recipes are ranges only.

To make cleanup easier, spray the inside of the Slow Cooker with non-stick cooking spray before adding food.

Meats will not brown in a Slow Cooker. If a recipes calls for meat to be browned, brown it in a skillet. The recipe will be better, it will enhance the flavor and decrease fat.

A Slow Cooker is great for tougher cuts of meat.

It is always better to thaw meat before placing it in the Slow Cooker. It will cook faster.

Fill cooker between half and two-thirds full.

Add vegetables to cooker first, then add meat. Vegetables cook slower than meat.

Cut vegetables in smaller pieces to ensure proper cooking.

Do not add as much water as regular recipes indicate. Use about half the recommended amount, unless it calls for rice or pasta. Liquids don't boil away as in conventional cooking.

If recipe calls for raw rice, add ¼ cup extra liquid per ¼ cup of raw rice

If recipe calls for pasta or rice, cook until slightly tender.

If recipe calls for dry beans, it is best to cook beans before adding to recipe.

In the last hour of cooking it is better to add milk, sour cream or cream to the recipe. Dairy products tend to curdle over long cooking periods. Condensed cream of soup or evaporated milk can be substituted in some recipes.

Processed cheeses tend to work better in Slow Cookers than natural cheese.

Juices can be thickened by adding corn starch during the last hour of cooking. Turn heat to high.

It is best to add ground seasoning near the end of cooking.

Cooking Guide for Adapting Recipes

BAKING TIMES	SLOW COOKER	SLOW COOKER
IF RECIPE SAYS COOK	COOK ON LOW	COOK ON HIGH
15 to 30 minutes	4 to 6 hours	1½ to 2 hours
35 to 45 minutes	6 to 10 hours	3 to 4 hours
50 minutes to 3 hours	8 to 15 hours	4 to 6 hours

SLOW COOKER DON'TS

• DON'T remove the lid during cooking unless recipe calls for it. Every time you lift the lid you will slow the cooking time by 20 to 30 minutes.

• DON'T leave food in the Crock Pot®. Remove food within one hour.

• DON'T reheat food in a Crock Pot® because it takes too much time for food to reach a safe temperature.

• DON'T add water to clean the cooker until it has cooled.

• DON'T use metal utensils; use rubber, plastic or wood to avoid damaging interior of the Crock Pot®s.

Herbs and Spices Are Used for What?

BASIL — Good with stews, roast beef, ground beef, lamb, fish, vegetables, and omelets.

BAY LEAVES — Has a pungent flavor. Good in seafood, stews, and vegetable dishes.

CARAWAY — Use in breads, soups, cakes, cheese, and sauerkraut.

CHIVES — Good in salads, fish, soups, and potatoes.

CILANTRO — Southwestern dishes, rice, beans, salads, fish, and chicken.

CURRY POWDER — A combination of spices that give a distinct flavor to meat, poultry, fish, and vegetables.

DILL — Both seeds and leaves may be used. Leaves can be used as a garnish or cooked with soup, fish, potatoes, and beans.

FENNEL — Has a hot, sweet flavor. Small quantities are used in pies and baked goods, and the leaves can be boiled with fish.

GINGER — It is a pungent root and is used in pickles, cakes, cookies, preserves, soups, and meat dishes.

MARJORAM — It adds flavor to stew, stuffing, lamb, fish, poultry, and omelets.

MINT — It is great in beverages, soup, peas, carrots, lamb, cheese, preserves and fruit desserts.

OREGANO — It can be used whole or ground, in pizza, tomato juice, fish, eggs, omelets, stew, gravy, poultry, and vegetables.

PAPRIKA — A bright red pepper that is used as a garnish for potatoes, salads, and eggs, and as a spice used in meat, vegetables, and soup.

PARSLEY — Can be used dried as seasoning or garnish. Use in fish, soup, meat, stuffing, and mixed greens.

ROSEMARY — It can be used to season fish, stuffing, beef, lamb, poultry, onions, eggs, bread, and potatoes. It is great in dressings.

SAFFRON — It is used in breads, soup, rice, and chicken.

SAGE — May be used in stuffing, fish, omelets, poultry, tomato juice, breads, and cheese spreads.

TARRAGON — Used in salads, sauces, fish, poultry, tomatoes, eggs, carrots, green beans, and dressing.

THYME — Leaves may be sprinkled on fish or poultry before baking or broiling.

Cooking Techniques

SEAR — To brown quickly over high heat

SAUTÉ — To fry lightly and quickly in a little hot oil while being frequently turned over.

ROAST — A dry-heat method of cooking meat or poultry in an oven.

BAKE — A dry heat for baking bread, pies or cake.

STEAM — To cook food over boiling water in a covered pan.

FRY — Pan frying is done in a small amount of oil. Deep frying is immersed in hot oil.

BOIL — To cook in liquid that is bubbling.

POACH — To gently cook in not quite simmering water or seasoned liquid.

GRILL — To cook on a grill or directly over an open flame.

Substitutions

OUT OF THIS INGREDIENT? THEN SUBSTITUTE:

INGREDIENT	AMOUNT	SUBSTITUTE
Allspice	1 teaspoon	½ teaspoon cinnamon and ½ teaspoon ground cloves
Baking Powder	1 teaspoon	¼ teaspoon baking soda and 1 teaspoon cream of tartar
Broth-beef or chicken	1 cup	1 bouillon cube dissolved in 1 cup boiling water
Catsup	1 cup	1 cup tomato sauce, ½ cup sugar and 2 teaspoons vinegar
Chives, finely chopped	2 teaspoons	2 teaspoons finely chopped green onion tips
Chocolate chips-semi sweet	1 ounce	1 ounce sweet cooking chocolate
Cornstarch-for thickening	1 tablespoon	2 tablespoons all-purpose flour 4 to 6 teaspoons quick cooking tapioca
Cracker Crumbs	¾ cup	1 cup bread crumbs
Cream Cheese	1 cup	cottage cheese beaten until smooth
Dry Mustard	1 teaspoon	1 tablespoon prepared mustard
Flour, cake	1 cup sifted	1 cup minus 2 teaspoons all-purpose flour
Flour, self rising	1 cup	1 cup minus 2 teaspoons all-purpose flour plus 1½ teaspoons baking powder and ½ teaspoon salt
Herbs, fresh	1 tablespoon	1 teaspoon dried herbs

INGREDIENT	AMOUNT	SUBSTITUTE
Milk, sour	1 cup	1 tablespoon lemon juice and 1 cup milk
Milk, buttermilk	1 cup	1 cup plain yogurt
Milk, whole	1 cup	½ cup evaporated milk
Onion, fresh	1 small	1 tablespoon minced onion, dehydrated
Sugar, brown	½ cup	2 tablespoons molasses in ½ cup granulated sugar
Sugar, confectioner's	1 cup	1 cup granulated sugar plus 1 teaspoon cornstarch
Sugar, maple	½ cup	1 cup maple syrup
Tomatoes, fresh	2 cups	1 (16 ounce) can diced tomatoes
Tomato sauce	1 (15-ounce) can	1 (6-ounce) can tomato paste plus cup water
Wine	1 cup	13 tablespoons water, 3 tablespoons lemon juice and 1 tablespoon sugar
Worcestershire sauce	1 teaspoon	1 teaspoon bottled steak sauce
Yogurt	1 cup	1 cup sour cream

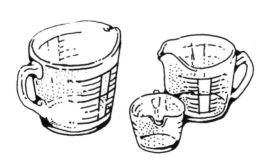

It Makes How Much?

FOOD FOR INGREDIENTS	QUANTITY	YIELDS
Apple	1 medium	1 cup
Bread Crumbs	1 slice	¼ cup
Butter	1 stick	½ cup
Egg whites	8 to 10	1 cup
Egg yolks	10 to 12	1 cup
Lemon	1 medium	3 tablespoons lemon juice
Noodles, uncooked	1½ cups	2 to 3 cups cooked
Macaroni, uncooked	1¼ cups	2½ cups cooked
Spaghetti	8 ounces	4½ cups cooked
Nuts, chopped	¼ pound	1 cup
Nuts, walnuts, unshelled	1 pound	1½ cups
Onion, chopped	1 medium	½ cup
Rice, regular	1 cup	3 cups cooked
Rice, wild	1 cup	4 cups cooked
Sugar, brown	1 pound	2½ cups
Sugar, white	1 pound	2 cups

Measurements For Cooking

3 teaspoons... 1 tablespoon

2 tablespoons..1 fluid ounce

4 tablespoons..¼ cup

5 tablespoons plus 1 teaspoon....................⅓ cup

8 tablespoons..½ cup

16 tablespoons.......................................1 cup

Dash...less than ⅛ teaspoon

Pinch...as much as can be taken between tip of fingers and thumb

Hints To Make Cooking Easy

1. If an egg cracks while being cooked in the shell, add a small amount of vinegar to the water to prevent the egg white from seeping from the shell.

2. Add 1 teaspoon of salt to cold water before boiling eggs to make them easier to peel.

3. Fresh lemon juice will remove onion scent form your hands.

4. Soak potatoes to be baked for 20 to 30 minutes to make them bake faster.

5. Freeze extra chopped onions, peppers and other vegetables for later use.

6. Marinate meat in sturdy plastic bag — no cleanup, no mess.

7. Use an egg slicer to quickly slice mushrooms

8. Keep knives sharp to reduce chopping time.

9. Spray the blade of the knife with cooking spray before cutting cheese or dried fruit. It will make cutting easier.

10. When measuring shortening, butter, etc., dip the spoon in hot water. The fat will slip out easily.

11. Cookie dough that is to be rolled is much easier to handle if it has been refrigerated for 15 to 30 minutes.

12. For scorched pans fill them halfway with water and ¼ cup baking soda. Boil until the burned portions loosen and float to the top.

13. Remove food burnt in a skillet by adding a drop of liquid dish soap, add water to fill halfway, bring to a boil.

14. Keep disinfecting wipes handy and clean as you cook.

Basic Rules For Good Manners At The Dinner Table

Civilization has taught us to eat with a fork, but even now if nobody is around, we use our fingers. — Will Rogers

THE NAPKIN

As soon as you are seated, put your napkin in your lap. If you are at a formal dinner, wait for the hostess to place hers on her lap first.

When the meal is finished put your napkin at the side of your plate. Do not crumple or refold your napkin – leave it on the table in loose folds.

WHICH SILVERWARE TO USE

Start at the left of your plate and work your way toward the plate with each course.

You should wait until everyone has been served before you start to eat.

When you have finished the main course, place the knife and fork beside each other on the dinner plate diagonally from the upper left to lower right, with the handles extending slightly over the plate.

BEVERAGE

Before you take a drink, blot your lips to help keep your beverage free of food particles.

Never leave your spoon in the coffee cup.

SOUP

When eating soup that is served in a bowl or soup dish, dip the soup spoon away from you, not toward you. If soup is served in a cup on a saucer, you can place the spoon on the plate and drink as you would a beverage.

PLEASE PASS

It is okay to reach for anything at the table unless you have to stretch across your neighbor, or lean too far across the table. When something is out of reach ask the person nearest to the item to pass it to you.

DESSERT

If dessert is served in a small deep bowl on another plate, place the dessert spoon on the plate when you are finished. If the bowl is shallow and wide the spoon may be left in it.

Mealtime Don'ts

- DON'T talk with your mouth full of food.
- DON'T take too large mouthfuls of any food.
- DON'T put a beverage into your mouth if it is filled with food
- DON'T cut up your entire meal before you start to eat. Don't wave your fork or spoon around during conversation.
- DON'T encircle the plate with your arm while eating.
- DON'T wipe off silverware in a restaurant. Ask for new ones.
- DON'T push your plate back when you are finished. Let it remain until your server removes it.
- DON'T Slurp.
- DON'T blow your nose at the dinner table.
- ALWAYS eat with your mouth closed.

Index

OTHER COOKBOOKS AVAILABLE FROM CREATIVE IDEAS PUBLISHING

To order, fill out enclosed order form.

BUSY WOMAN'S COOKBOOK A national bestseller by Sharon and Gene McFall. Over 350,000 copies sold. It has over 500 mouth-watering 3 and 4 ingredient recipes and more than 200 short stories and facts about famous and influential women. $16.95

COOKIN' WITH WILL ROGERS by Sharon and Gene McFall. Has over 560 delicious country cookin' recipes with over 100 Will Rogers quotes, 60 pictures and 50 stories of one of America's most beloved humorists. "Only a fool argues with a skunk, a mule or a cook." Will Rogers. $19.95.

HOME MADE BLESSINGS by Diane Reasoner. Over 400 excellent tasting recipes, straight forward instructions and ingredients that are found in any pantry. Inspirational sayings on every page that will brighten your day. $19.95.

MILD TO WILD MEXICAN COOKBOOK by Linda Burgett. Over 400 tantalizing recipes from south of the border. Every recipe tells you if it is hot, medium or mild-so you have no big surprises. Also has fun facts on ingredients. One word for this book—Wonderful. $18.95.

GET ME OUT OF THE KITCHEN by Sharon and Gene McFall. 500 easy to prepare recipes. Special low-fat and low-cal recipes as well as helpful cooking hints. A wonderful cookbook. $18.95.

JUST AROUND THE CURVE by Sharon and Gene McFall. Designed for RVers and Campers, but is great for the home. Over 350 great quick and easy recipes. Recipes from all 50 states. Also contains some low-fat, low-cal and diabetic recipes. Intriguing American points of interest and travel tips and tidbits. A must for the traveler or at home. $16.95.

COMING

JUST NO TIME TO COOK! By Linda Burgett. Over 500 short cut recipes. Delicious and quick to make with ingredients that are found in any kitchen. It also has special recipes and great ideas for the holidays, plus tips to greatly cut your cleaning time. This cookbook will simplify your life in the kitchen, around the house and during the holidays. $18.95

Please send _____ copies of _____

@ _____ (U.S.) each $_____

Postage and handling @ $3.50 each $_____

Texas residents add sales tax @ $1.69 each $_____

TOTAL $_____

Check or Credit Card (Canada-credit card only)

Charge to my ☐ Master Card or Visa Card

account # _____

expiration date _____

signature _____

<table>
<tr><td>MAIL TO:
Cookbooks by Shelley
P.O. Box 14932
Tallahassee, FL
32317-4932</td></tr>
</table>

Name _____

Address _____

City _____ State _____ Zip _____

Phone (day) _____ (night) _____

ORDER BY EMAIL: cookbooksbyshelley@yahoo.com

— —

Please send _____ copies of *If I Gotta Cook Make It Quick*

@ $18.95 (U.S.) each $_____

Postage and handling @ $3.50 each $_____

Texas residents add sales tax @ $1.69 each $_____

TOTAL $_____

Check or Credit Card (Canada-credit card only)

Charge to my ☐ Master Card or Visa Card

account # _____

expiration date _____

signature _____

<table>
<tr><td>MAIL TO:
Cookbooks by Shelley
P.O. Box 14932
Tallahassee, FL
32317-4932</td></tr>
</table>

Name _____

Address _____

City _____ State _____ Zip _____

Phone (day) _____ (night) _____

ORDER BY EMAIL: cookbooksbyshelley@yahoo.com

SHARE YOUR FAVORITE RECIPE

Do you have a favorite quick and easy recipe? Do family and friends ask you for it? Would you like to see it in a national cookbook?

If so, please send your favorite quick and easy recipe to us. If we use it in a future cookbook, you will be given credit in the book for the recipe, and will receive a free copy of the book.

Submit to: Creative Ideas Publishing
             PMB 115
             7916 N.W. 23rd Street
             Bethany, OK 73003-5135